Julia-
I look forward to working with you. Keep that spark! And always give......

My Orange Best,

GRACED WITH ORANGE

GRACED WITH ORANGE

how caring for cambodia
changed lives, including my own

JAMIE C. AMELIO

written with Adam Snyder

MEADOW LANE PUBLISHING

Austin, TX

Published by
Meadow Lane Publishing
Austin, TX

Publisher's Cataloging-in-Publication Data
Amelio, Jamie C.

Graced with orange : how Caring for Cambodia changed lives, including my own/ by Jamie C. Amelio, written with Adam Snyder. – Austin, TX : Meadow Lane Pub., 2013.

p. ; cm.

ISBN13: 978-0-9860258-0-8

1. Caring for Cambodia (Organization)—History. 2. Poor children—Education—Cambodia. 3. Poor children—Cambodia—Social conditions. 4. Charities—Cambodia. 5. Amelio, Jamie C. I. Title. II. Snyder, Adam.

LA1191.A64 2013
370.9596—dc23   2012950839

Project coordination by Jenkins Group, Inc.
www.BookPublishing.com

Interior design by Brooke Camfield

Printed in the United States of America
17 16 15 14 13 • 5 4 3 2 1

Caring for Cambodia
Mission Statement

A t Caring for Cambodia our goal is to secure a better, brighter future for the children of Cambodia through education. How?

By building schools that stand up to world-class standards. By investing in our teaching staff, training them, and empowering them to be mentors.

Caring for Cambodia provides educational opportunities for Cambodian children so they may reach their highest potential and make valuable contributions to their communities. We work to educate one child at a time today to make a difference for Cambodia's tomorrow.

A portion of the proceeds from the sale of this book will be donated to Caring for Cambodia.

Contents

Acknowledgments

Caring for Cambodia, and therefore this book, would not exist but for the hundreds of volunteers who have donated so much of their time, energy, efforts, and in many cases their hearts and souls to our united cause. I am in awe of their dedication and commitment. I thank each and every one of you.

I intended to include a list in the appendix of all our contributors, foundation supporters, corporate sponsors, and sister schools, but the list has become so long and fluid that it became an impossible task. But they know who they are and that the CFC schools in Siem Reap would never have been been built without their help.

I will also be forever grateful to my loving husband Bill for helping my dream become a reality. He walked beside me, never held me back, and was my rock of support and encouragement. He has become so orange that sometimes I think he forgets which of his jobs he is talking about.

Caring for Cambodia has become a part of his corporate world, just like it became part of our family. Together, Bill and I have been the yin and yang of so many things in our life together. CFC allowed us to learn and grow in ways we never could have imagined.

To him, to our children Avery, Bronson, Riley, Rathana, Cherry, and Austin, and to the children of Cambodia, I dedicate this book.

Writing a book is a difficult thing. Writing a book about such deep emotion is even harder. I found friends and foes along the way, and I forged a friendship I never expected. Adam Snyder and his wife Pat stood beside me on this journey of putting it all on paper. Adam cared about every word and helped me like no one else could have. I am forever "orangely" grateful to my friends for life.

Author's Note

I will never forget my first orange moment, standing on the back side of Angkor Wat, those majestic temples in Siem Reap, Cambodia. Four or five monks in their bright orange robes were walking across the lush, rain-soaked fields when just then a waif of a girl tugged at my shirt, asking in English if she could have a dollar. Little did I know, but that was the birth of Caring for Cambodia.

Being orange is an expression I later coined to refer to individuals—good and kind people—who get what we are trying to do in Siem Reap. I have repeatedly witnessed peoples' inner light magically turn this brilliant hue when they walk into our schoolyards or classrooms, hold the hand of a young Cambodian student, or congratulate an older youth with a smile. People feel it, and they become committed members of Caring for Cambodia, spreading the word about us and volunteering an extraordinary amount of their time helping to educate the children of Cambodia, a country where, in the 1970s, teachers were deliberately singled out and murdered by the Khmer Rouge.

I knew the word *orange* had to be in the title of this book, but we went through a dozen names, including *Beyond Orange, The Orange Promise*, and *Becoming Orange.* We even got silly with titles like *Orange You Glad I Didn't Say Banana?* until *Graced with Orange* came to mind. It immediately felt right.

The Cambridge online dictionary defines the verb *grace* as "to honor people by taking part in something." I feel graced to have had Caring for Cambodia and the children of Cambodia come into my life and into the life of my family.

Jamie Amelio

December, 2012

PROLOGUE

Virginia

Spring break 2010. After almost a decade in Singapore I was coming home to Austin, Texas, with my fourteen-year-old son Riley to get the house ready for my family to move in two months later. And to see Virginia.

Virginia was my best friend in the world. During my decade in Asia I don't think three days ever went by that we didn't talk on the phone. I was twenty-one when we first met, living in Austin, and I didn't know anything. My dad had died when I was seventeen and shortly after that my mother took off to England to care for her family there. I guess you could say I was *look'n for love.*

I married at nineteen. Kenny was older; he had gone to our rival high school in Converse, Texas. He was gorgeous, popular, and very funny, always the life of the party. I worked and went to school until our son Austin was born. I was just twenty-two. Our marriage was full of late night partying and a lifestyle I knew I did not want to be around, and more importantly, did not want my son to be around. Kenny and I separated when Austin was two and divorced a short while later. I struggled during those years, a single parent with an ex-husband who barely paid child support.

When I met Virginia I had just married Kenny and would soon be pregnant with Austin. Virginia was eighteen years older than I was and she quickly became someone I looked up to. She talked to me about what I would experience having and caring for a baby, and we had long discussions about marriage and what it meant to be a good mother, daughter, and friend.

Oh how I wanted to be like her; she was so giving and genuine. I always thought I was too young and not smart or sophisticated enough for the "Virginia group." But she believed in me, and in the next few years she gave me the courage to face a tough world with a smile on my face. She helped me through a difficult divorce and taught me to stand on my own two feet.

A quarter of a century later my life had changed profoundly. I was happily married to Bill Amelio, and together we had six wonderful kids. 2010 marked the end of an era for me and my family and the beginning of a new adventure. Back home in Texas, I would be 10,000 miles away, operating Caring for Cambodia (CFC), the organization I had founded that had built sixteen schools in Siem Reap, Cambodia, trained hundreds of teachers, and become such an important part of my life and the life of my family.

For more than two decades, the one constant in my life had always been Virginia. When things were crazy with my son Austin, or when making CFC a success seemed overwhelming, Virginia was always there for me, a shoulder to lean on.

Riley, Virginia, and I went to dinner that Sunday night during spring break to celebrate Riley's fourteenth birthday. Virginia looked great and so happy. We drank wine and laughed all through dinner. Riley loved her too. She took her job as his godmother very seriously. When she came to North Carolina to see us a few days after he was born she marched right in and said, "Give me that baby," and started talking to him as if they had been friends for years.

Virginia and Riley, 1997.

After dinner we stood in the parking lot and said our goodbyes. But we never really said goodbye. We used to tell each other, "I'm not saying goodbye because I'm always coming right back." So we hugged and said, "I love you and I'll see you in a bit." Little did I know that was the last time we would hug standing up.

Two days later Riley and I were on a plane back to Singapore. I called Virginia as soon as I landed. She said she had a bit of a cold, but was otherwise fine. That was Thursday. I didn't talk to her Friday because she was going to a funeral. When we spoke on Saturday she didn't sound right.

Sunday she answered her phone but said she would call me back. She didn't. I tried calling all day on Monday but got no answer. Tuesday night her daughter, Amanda, called from the hospital and told me her mom had pneumonia and was really sick. I kept my phone with me every minute until Amanda called again, crying, and said she needed me. I got on the next plane out. Singapore to Austin takes about twenty-five hours. I arrived at about 11:00 p.m. on Wednesday and took a taxi right to the hospital.

> *Virginia is in intensive care, on a ventilator, a nurse is hovering. When someone is dying they hardly leave them alone. Amanda is here with me. I can't leave. I just can't believe it; Virginia is so sick. I am more jetlagged than I've ever been, after two twenty-four-hour flights within a week. Now I really don't know what time zone I'm in. I keep thinking, "How on earth does Bill travel back and forth like this?" I run home to take a quick shower and come right back to the hospital.*
>
> *The next few days are filled with loving friends of Virginia's, praying, waiting, laughing, hoping, and not leaving Virginia or Amanda alone. Good Friday I go to church to pray. It's just one big huge "Come on, please don't take her now." I beg God not to take my friend.*
>
> *Back at the hospital I hear the nurse, Sheila, tell Amanda to prepare herself. I sit frozen. Amanda gets up and rubs her mom's knees, bends down, stands up, pushes her hair back, and says, "NO, I need her. What about my wedding? My children? She can't leave; there has to be something we can do. Someone has to know how to help her."*

I stare at Virginia in that bed. She would hate the way her hair looks; she would want some kind of makeup. This is not a good thing. I hold her hand. The room is supposed to remain sterile, but the nurses have stopped reminding us. This alone is wrong, another hit of reality. I stare hard at Virginia. Come on. Something . . . just something.

Easter Sunday I call the priest. He comes to the hospital on the busiest, most important day of the Catholic religion. Really? He comes, we pray over Virginia, he puts the oil on her head. I know this is it. Or do I really? Surely she will come out of this, right? It's Easter. He gave us one gift; might He give us another? That night we take turns sleeping in the bed beside her. Amanda, Amanda's boyfriend Bob, a professional singer, and me. Everyone else has left for the night.

Amanda hasn't given up. She calls everyone she knows, exhausts every possibility to save her mother. Such admiration I have for her. The love is hanging on; the strongest bond there could ever be between two people is being tested, stretched. The pain I feel just seeing this is unbearable. I have not slept for days and days.

In addition to the pain, I am feeling an enormous amount of responsibility for doing what Virginia would want me to do. Take care of her daughter, let her friends know, plan. Oh God, she is really going to leave me. Almost every day for the last twenty-three years I have talked to her and she is really leaving.

The space age bed rotates to take pressure off the lungs. It's Amanda's call to once again turn her, suspend her, relieve the fluid in her lungs, all for naught. Virginia's system is shutting down.

Monday morning Amanda goes home with Bob to shower. Dr. Shapiro comes in while I am sleeping beside Virginia but I immediately open my eyes and stand up. I watch him look at all the equipment. He shakes his head, turns to the nurse, and says something. He walks around her, looking at the blinking machines and shakes his head again. I hold myself up by leaning against the wall. He looks straight at me and tells me, "No, she is not going to live." I feel my back melt into the wall. I slide down and try to catch my breath and to get it together but I'm frozen for several seconds, unable to breathe. I look him straight in the eye and ask, "Are you sure?" He says yes.

Be strong, I keep telling myself. All right, so how is this going to go down? I ask the doctor to tell me the least amount of pain she will have to endure. Amanda's friend Kimmy is in the room too, listening. Suddenly I feel like mama bear. I don't want Amanda to see her mom suffer with her last breath.

I drive to Virginia's house and sit in front of Amanda and tell her what will happen. She picks out a gorgeous cream silk dress and together we find her mom's best silk bedding. We take Virginia's favorite scarves for all of us to wear.

Back at the hospital the nurses prepare Virginia. Those of us who dearly love her are beside her. Amanda, Brittany, Candy, Debby, Sheila, Staci, Tiffany, and me. Bob plays her favorite songs on his guitar, "Bottom of the Big Blue Sea" and "Somewhere Over the Rainbow."

Amanda pulls the covers over her mom and climbs up beside her on the bed. My heart feels like it has been crushed and my bones ache. I'm silently gasping for air, telling myself to breathe. Be strong. I need to be strong for Virginia, and for her daughter.

I kiss Virginia and tell her I love her. This time it is goodbye. The machines are all shut off except the heart monitor. Seconds later it beeps. I look at the nurse and he nods his head. "Amanda honey," I say, "she's gone."

On Tuesday I call my youngest, five-year-old Avery who I call my angel. She tells me that Virginia is now the angel.

Virginia's death forced me to look at life without a filter. How do you go from talking to someone every day to suddenly knowing you never will never speak to her again? I still catch myself imagining telling her about my day.

The service was held in Austin the following Friday, April 9, on my seventeenth wedding anniversary. On that beautiful spring day we released butterflies as a sign of rebirth, but mostly to express what our souls were feeling. An unexpected tranquility filled me as I thought about a day seven years earlier, during my first trip to Cambodia, when Virginia and I saw butterflies at another place where the heart ached.

ONE

Spotting the Orange

Naturally, Virginia was with me in January of 2003 when I stepped off the plane in Siem Reap for the first time, the day that would change my life. As the airplane door banged open, Virginia, Amanda, and I felt the same blast of furnace-like air. When someone asks you what Cambodia is like, if you're honest, the first thing that comes to mind is, "Cambodia is hot." Jungle hot. If you start traveling to Cambodia frequently you are bound to hear the joke that everyone seems to tell: Cambodia has three seasons—hot, really hot, and really hot and wet.

Maybe so, but as a Texas girl I wasn't afraid of the heat *or* the rain. Having visited other Asian countries, I was also prepared for the chaos of traffic jams, honking horns, and swarms of children asking for, and sometimes demanding, money.

When you become an expatriate living in Singapore your new friends tell you to take the opportunity to explore neighboring countries like Thailand, Vietnam, Cambodia, and Hong Kong, all a few hours or fewer away by air.

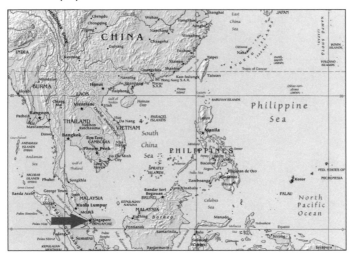

Map of Singapore in Asia.

During our first year in Singapore Bill and I traveled to a number of different countries, including China when Bill had business there, plus Thailand, Indonesia, and Hong Kong either with friends or our children. On one vacation Bill and I took the kids to Ho Chi Minh City, so I had experienced the ferocity and commercialism of a Southeast Asian capital. The children there were a reflection of this aggressiveness, and as soon as we arrived at the airport we were bombarded with swarms of them crying out to me, "Hey lady! Hey lady!" as they begged for money.

We did have a fascinating few days in Ho Chi Minh City. We visited museums, saw a water puppet show, and toured the incredible Củ Chi tunnels, an immense network of underground tunnels used by the Viet Cong army during the Vietnam War, or "the American War" as the Vietnamese call it.

We also brought clothes to donate to one of the orphanages Christina Noble had created. I had been moved to tears reading Ms. Noble's book,

Bridge Across My Sorrows, a memoir chronicling her horrific childhood in the slums of Dublin and how she had moved to Vietnam and devoted her life to the *bui doi*, the street children there. Her book was no doubt one of the inspirations that made me on the lookout for some way to make a positive difference in one of these very poor countries in Southeast Asia, located just a few hours from where I was now living.

I wanted to help, but as Bill and I visited one of the orphanages Ms. Noble had established, I immediately saw I would have to get involved in something very different. Looking at the conditions in which children were living left me dumfounded. We saw horribly deformed young people. Many children, some in diapers, seemed unable to even get out of bed. My most haunting memory is of the silence. We never heard the sounds of children playing or even crying. I greatly admired the people working there, but I left feeling devastated by the experience. I didn't think I was strong enough to work in that kind of environment.

But right away Siem Reap seemed different. The airport had an unexpected calm. It would be modernized a few years later, but at the time it resembled a Pony Express outpost more than it did the second largest airport in a country of fifteen million people. As Virginia, Amanda, and I deplaned and walked across the runway we saw green vegetation that seemed to go on forever and tall palm trees and grass huts in the distance. It was as if we were walking around someone's remote backyard.

As we were driven to our hotel, the city seemed to be moving at a slower pace. The streets were certainly crowded, but with motorbikes and bicycles rather than the constant hum of automobiles and twenty-first century neon and without the high-octane energy I had expected.

So this is what a developing country looks like, I thought to myself as I gazed at cows, monkeys, and dogs roaming the streets and at dirt flying everywhere. Driving alongside us, families carried all manner of things on their bicycles and motorbikes: babies on handlebars, bags of rice strapped to shoulders, pigs being taken to slaughter in cages dangling precariously from saddlebags. Many motorbikes carted three or four people in addition to their various belongings. No one wore helmets.[1]

We sped past villages with barefoot children playing in the mud, not an electric pole in sight. Somehow the large buildings and modern activity in the other Southeast Asian countries I had visited had managed to mask the impoverishment, at least for the tourist. In Siem Reap, it was all in your face.

I felt like I had been dropped down the rabbit hole, except it was a familiar one, like a vaguely scary dream but one I didn't fear because I'd had it before and I knew it came out okay on the other side. Instantly I felt comfortable in Siem Reap. My connection to the place went beyond just an empathy for people living in poverty. Even before we arrived at the hotel, well before we visited the temples, something struck a nerve in me. It's difficult to explain. Some people fall in love at first sight with Paris or New York; others feel a special affinity for the big sky of the American West or even the small towns of Texas where I grew up. Almost immediately I had the powerful feeling that Cambodia was a place that was going to become an important part of my life. Maybe it was the way people greeted us, with a slight bow as they put their hands together up to their chins in a prayer-like motion. It was a salutation I would soon adopt. Or perhaps it was the simplicity of their lives and the feeling that it wouldn't take much to make a genuine and lasting difference here.

The Raffles Hotel presented a wake-up of a different sort. Today Siem Reap has dozens of quality hotels, but at the time Raffles was the only one of its kind. It is still an oasis of beauty, one of the most elegant hotels I've

---

1. A few years later the police began to enforce a helmet law for motorbikes, but the law applies only to the driver. You can still routinely see three or four people on the same small bike, with only the driver wearing a helmet.

ever stayed in. The employees wear stiffly starched white uniforms with traditional hats and matching knee socks and offer a cold washcloth and a soft "Welcome home" as you walk through the door. The experience, walking out of poverty and into luxury, is surreal and more than a little disconcerting.

The next morning Samedi, the guide we had hired, picked up Virginia, Amanda, and me in his beat-up Toyota to visit the temple of Angkor Wat, the most famous of the temples of Angkor. On the way we passed King Jayaraman Hospital, named for the Khmer emperor who in the twelfth century built his capital city less than a mile from the entrance to the temple.

Outside the hospital a long snaking line of people waited to enter. There must have been several hundred tired, sick-looking men, women, and children waiting in line or on the street corner hoping to see a doctor. Many were parents holding ailing babies or toddlers; others were sick children holding even sicker younger siblings.

I started grilling Samedi, who explained that families travel on foot, by bicycle, and on the backs of trucks from their villages many hours away to see the only doctor for a hundred miles. With the exception of the cities of Siem Reap and Phnom Penh, modern healthcare in Cambodia is almost nonexistent, which helps explain why dengue fever and malaria continue to be major health problems.

Healthcare is not free in Cambodia. With an average income of $1,800 per year, many families must fend for themselves, often using ancient remedies of dubious efficacy, like squeezing someone's ankle if you think he's having a heart attack, or rubbing heated bottle tops or coins on the skin to "get the sickness out." It took me years to ask what caused the round marks on people's foreheads. I have also seen medicine men mix up a "cure your cancer" cocktail made of wood chips, herbs, and magic.

After just a few hours I could see that Cambodia was a country of paradoxes. Something beautiful like the fountains in the Raffles hotel existed just down the road from an entire village lacking plumbing or electricity. Temples built in the twelfth century, truly a wonder of the world, sat next to a hospital full of dying children who would not see a doctor until it was too late. The manmade magnificence of the ancient temples were in stark contrast to the manmade destitution in people's daily lives; the gentle, soft-spoken people I met during my first 48 hours there lived with the memory of a genocide the rest of the world had all but forgotten.

Even the restaurants demonstrated the yin/yang of the small city. You might enter a dining place with an attractive, modern façade, but a glance next door would reveal dogs and birds rummaging through the restaurant's burning garbage. Attempts at progress were butting up against years of extreme poverty and political upheaval, preventing people from making real progress.

Only later did I come to understand that Cambodian culture had recently been rebooted. Everywhere, in the eyes of the people and in their halting attempts to improve their lot, were remembrances of the recent past and the genocide they had endured. During my first days in Siem Reap I only had a cursory knowledge of what the Khmer Rouge had done to this beautiful country. I immediately started reading all I could about it, and what I learned was horrifying.

Between 1975 and 1979, in the name of creating an agrarian utopia, the Khmer Rouge had killed an estimated two million Cambodians, a quarter of the population, in a wave of murder, torture, and starvation aimed particularly at the educated and intellectual elite. Ninety percent of Cambodia's doctors were either killed or fled the country. Small wonder that even today, Cambodia has fewer physicians per capita than all but thirty-seven countries in the world and an infant mortality rate more than ten times that of the United States and almost six times that of neighboring Vietnam. If a U.S. tourist becomes ill during a vacation to Cambodia, the CDC (Centers for Disease Control) recommends air-lifting the patient to Bangkok rather than gambling with a Cambodian hospital or doctor.

It wasn't just modern medicine that the Khmer Rouge leadership considered subversive, antithetical to their rural, "pure" form of communism. In 1976, a year after taking power, the Khmer Rouge, formally the Communist Party of Kampuchea (CPK), abolished the Cambodian currency, the courts, newspapers, the postal system, and telephone communication—in short, the very concept of urban life.

Phnom Phen, a city of three million, was emptied, the people forced to work in the countryside or worse, never heard from again. The "revolution" led by Pol Pot wasn't just an attempt to eliminate disparities in income, monopolize the media, or limit personal freedoms. Individual thought, initiative, and creativity were also condemned. Anyone who was educated, particularly teachers, were targeted. People were shot simply because they wore glasses.

Angkor Wat

Virginia, Amanda, and I weren't thinking about any of this as we entered the grounds of Angkor Wat, surely one of the wonders of the ancient world. The temple was built during the Khmer Empire between the ninth and thirteenth centuries when Cambodian kings ruled a Southeast Asian empire that stretched from Malaysia to Laos, from Vietnam to Burma.

Sometime during the first half of the twelfth century the emperor Suryavarman II dedicated Angkor Wat to the Hindu God, Vishnu. Every inch of the temple seems to be made with purpose. The intricate statues and sculptures that appear to climb out of the walls and rock cliffs give reverence to both Hindu and Buddhist deities and emperors, and numerology is interwoven throughout. In Hinduism, the God-like *Devas* are continually at war with the power-seeking deities called *Asuras*. The bridge that leads to Angkor Thom, which is part of Angkor Wat, is lined with 54 rivaling *Devas* and a corresponding 54 *Asura* statues. Together they add up to 108, a powerful number in Khmer mythology that is linked to the degrees of movement of the sun and moon.

Approaching the temple on foot makes you feel as if you are in a Tolkien land with ancient trees growing in and over the roads and buildings. The jungle heat prints the landscape green and emits a fresh smell of life regenerating. The rhythm and beauty of my first day in Cambodia were almost overpowering.

Seven Amelios at the Angkor Wat South Gate entrance; a tuk-tuk is on the left.

The First Orange I See

At one point we were walking around the side of the temples and we could see in the distance four or five Buddhist monks in bright orange robes heading toward a nearby monastery. Just then a little girl of eight or nine came up to us. Throughout the day children had been asking us to buy all sorts of items. Each child seemed to have a specialty. Some sold silk scarves, others postcards and maps, still others books describing local tourist sites.

But there was something different about this girl who offered me a book on Angkor Wat and asked for a dollar. She approached us by herself, surrounded only by a flock of wild puppies running and yelping around her. In a soft clear voice, she asked, "How are you?"

At the time I was surprised at her ability to speak English, but I soon learned that most of the children who work near the temples learn to speak at least a little English so they can converse with the tourists.

"Could I have a dollar?" this sweet small voice asked.

Rather than just give her the money, I asked for her name and what she would do with the dollar. I wanted to understand what was going on in her country. That I didn't know very much about Cambodia was beginning to dawn on me. It was poor; I could certainly see that after half a day. It had been part of the Vietnam War somehow, I remembered that. And the country had suffered through a genocide of its own making less than thirty years earlier. But what had happened since then, I hadn't a clue.

The girl told me her name was Srelin and that she wanted the dollar to pay for school.

"What a clever answer," I thought suspiciously, imagining a street person in a U.S. city standing outside a liquor store asking for money, supposedly for food. Still, something about the girl's youth and her matter-of-factness captivated me.

"Why do you have to pay to go to school?" I asked her.

"We all have to pay to go to school in Cambodia," was the response.

"What does your mom do?"

"My mom can't work. She sick."

"Where's your father?"

"Well, he at home."

"Where do you get your money, here at the temple?"

"Yes."

I found myself telling Srelin that if she showed me her school I would give her the dollar. I fully expected her to tell me I wasn't allowed at the school, or to offer some other excuse. Instead she said that school wasn't in session since it was lunchtime, but that I could visit later that afternoon. Then, very businesslike, we shook hands.

On our way back from Angkor Wat I began pummeling our guide with more questions. Up until that point Samedi had been playing the good tour guide, telling us about the likes of King Jayaraman and the history of the various Hindu and Buddhist temples we would be visiting. Now I began asking him why his country was so poor, why children had to pay to go to school, and why Srelin's parents weren't working.

"What is the source of most families' income?" I asked. "Do they have electricity? Indoor plumbing?"

"Tourism," "No," and "No," I gradually gleaned were the answers to those three questions. A child under the age of ten serving as the family's breadwinner was not unusual, Samedi told me, and most homes did not have electricity. More than once since then I have seen people use a car battery to fire up a television set. On many nights that is the only light you see in a village.

"But what happened to this country?" I demanded. Vietnam and Thailand had developed into tiger economies. Why had Cambodia lagged seriously behind, with the lowest GDP in Asia?

Poor Samedi. He couldn't answer most of my questions, but he did talk about the infamous Killing Fields of Cambodia and what had happened to his country during the past thirty years.

"Almost everyone has a family member who was killed," he told me.

And everyone had a story, I was soon to learn. It was years before Samedi opened up and told me his. Eventually I learned that he was born in 1964, so he was eleven years old when the Khmer Rouge took power. Like millions of other peasants, he was marched out of his village and into forced labor in the countryside. Seven days a week he worked in the fields, from daybreak until ten at night, farming, herding cows, and building dikes. Virtually no one went to school. His was a story that was repeated a million times. All his family's belongings had to be handed over to the Khmer Rouge, the ruling Cambodian party which became everyone's mother, father, and big brother. If you were caught hiding jewelry you could be killed. If you tried to escape, you were killed.

In 1980 Samedi was reunited with his mother and other surviving family members, but his father, he learned, had been executed. Two of his siblings had also died. Samedi was then conscripted into the Vietnamese army and later saved himself by becoming a monk before leaving the monastery to make his way as a tour guide.

After lunch Samedi drove Virginia, Amanda, and me to Srelin's school in the small village of Kravaan. A large, rusty wrought iron fence with yellow columns buttressing a swinging metal gate led to a complex of three buildings, one of which was a small, low-roofed, shack-like structure. Somehow Srelin knew I had arrived because out the door she came running up to us, exclaiming, "Oh, you're here! You're here!" like I was a favorite aunt she hadn't seen in months.

I asked Srelin to show us her classroom, so she walked us back into the building, which up close we could see wasn't much more than four walls and a ceiling. She opened the door to reveal what must have been seventy-five children of all ages crammed into a small room. They were sitting on benches under narrow tables, three to five kids to a table. The school was so crowded that children were literally sitting on top of one another. Every time a child stood the dust from the dirt floor billowed upwards. I had to force myself to stop thinking about the *Peanuts* character Pigpen, trailed by a cloud of dirt wherever he went.

Thousands of dust particles sparkled in the rays of sun that shone through the windows, unobstructed except for thick steel bars. I was told the bars were to prevent break-ins, although what someone might want to steal I couldn't imagine. Even with the bars the building didn't seem particularly secure. I wondered how children could learn in this jail-like setting and marveled at the irony that they had to pay for it.

The moment I walked into the room the children went completely silent, with all eyes on the three foreigners. I said hello and they bowed their heads, offering polite "Hellos" in return.

Looking around further, I realized there wasn't a teacher in front of the class. "Where's the teacher?" I asked Srelin.

"I don't know if teacher come today. Sometimes don't come."

Remarkably, without supervision, the children just sat there, talking quietly, waiting for their teacher to arrive. Srelin explained that they would stay there all day because that's what they had been told to do.

"Do you have any kind of workbooks to read or lesson plans to follow while the teacher is absent?" I asked Srelin.

She looked at me blankly, but the fact that she didn't understand the question gave me my answer.

"Where are the school supplies?"

She pointed to the front desk, which had small pieces of broken pencils. "We get one pencil," she told me. "We break it. We share it."

The teacher never did show up that day. Virginia, Amanda, and I stayed a few hours, walking the grounds with the school principal. With Samedi as translator, I asked how I could help.

"What do you need the most?" I asked.

"Paper and pencils," the principal told me. I kept asking him questions, and in return I received my first introduction to the Cambodian public education system. It wasn't the last time I would learn that the bureaucracy was sorely inefficient and often corrupt. Teachers, I learned, were supposed to receive a salary from the Cambodian government. Sometimes they did, often they did not, and even when they did it only amounted to about $25 a month. That was not a livable wage, even in a country as poor as Cambodia, so the teachers asked the children to supplement their incomes.

By the time we returned to our hotel something in me had changed. My heart and head had been turned topsy-turvy in a single day. I couldn't sleep that night. Perhaps I was naïve, but I couldn't get my mind around the idea that I lived two hours away in a country with everything I could possibly need while a mere two hours away children were trying to learn in an environment like the one I had just seen. This was simply not okay with me. People could do better. People like *me* could do better.

The next day after breakfast Virginia, Amanda, and I visited another top tourist sight, Ta Prohm, the temple made famous by Angelina Jolie's film, *Lara Croft: Tomb Raider*.

Ta Prohm was built in the twelfth century, toward the end of the Khmer Empire. Although it retains its incredible beauty, it is losing its form to the jungle, crumbling under the weight of the massive trees and roots that snake between the stones, separating and lifting them in odd directions, filling every nook and cranny and giving the temple a Dali-like quality. Man conquered nature in its construction and now nature is reclaiming her temple.

Just before arriving at Ta Prohm, with Samedi still our guide, we stopped at a small outdoor market. Young girls were selling cold drinks and souvenirs out of a series of stalls protected from the sun by make-shift roofs and awnings stuffed with straw, leaves, and mud. Suddenly we were surrounded by a swarm of girls maybe twelve or thirteen years old. I bought a few souvenirs from them, but after my experience of the day before I had more questions.

"What school do you go to?" I asked. "Does your teacher always show up? Do you use books and pencils and paper at your school?"

Like Srelin, these young girls attended school most days and sold trinkets at Ta Prohm to pay for it. I took a photograph of the girls and wrote down their names so I wouldn't forget. We sat sipping water, talking for hours, and they told me a little about how they lived and pointed out their houses in a village without electricity. I asked about the sugar canes they were cleaning, and one of the girls pointed to a field full of them. All the girls chewed constantly on the cane, which explained their bad teeth.

Perhaps it was the water, but that night at Raffles both Virginia and I were so sick we had a doctor come and give us shots. The next morning, fighting through the nausea, I managed to meet with Samedi in the hotel lobby. I was obsessed with doing something to help, and I decided to give him $300 in cash, telling him I wanted to start helping the children of Cambodia by sponsoring the schooling of five girls—Srelin and a friend of hers I had met at her school plus the three girls I had sat with across from Ta Prohm.

Samedi was reluctant to take the money. I could see the apprehension on his face, as if to say, "Oh no, another tourist with big ideas who I'll never see again."

But I assured him I'd be back. I was adamant about giving this money to the girls and letting them know I'd be returning soon.

I know this sounds crazy as I barely knew Samedi, but a bigger plan was beginning to formulate in my mind. I wanted to establish that if I said I was going to do something I would follow through and do it. If I were truly going to do something in Cambodia I needed to create trust. I had promised each of these five girls the day I met them that I would help them, and I was going to start by making it possible for Srelin and the others to go to school for the next few months without having to pay for it. In the meantime, I was going to figure out a more permanent way to get involved.

That afternoon Virginia, Amanda, and I flew to Phnom Penh, Cambodia's capital. We still didn't feel well, and after we landed Virginia threw up on our way to the hotel, right in front of the Royal Palace.

I wondered if this was some kind of omen. As time has shown, the answer was a resounding no.

TWO

Lessons in Phnom Penh

P*hnom Penh,* Cambodia's largest city, was founded in 1434 on the banks of the Mekong River. It has been Cambodia's capital ever since the king of the Khmer Empire moved it there after Angkor Thom was captured by Siam.

By the 1920s Phnom Penh was considered the most beautiful of the Indochinese French-built cities, earning it the moniker "the Pearl of Asia." Today it still has its charms, including French boulevards and art deco architecture, highlighted by the Royal Palace and Phsar Thmei, once the largest market in Asia.

But as I entered the city for the first time all I could see was the contrast between Phnom Penh and the comparatively sleepy Siem Reap. In Siem Reap it is forbidden to build any structure higher than the temple of Angkor Wat, so you'll see no skyscrapers and its urban center is like a small windswept Texas town. Phnom Penh is much more of a metropolis, with a population of more than two million crammed inside its small urban streets. It has more crime, and its most extreme poverty is hidden in the back alleyways. Like Hanoi or Bangkok, visiting Phnom Penh makes you feel like you are rubbing shoulders with the entire country.

While in Phnom Penh I devoured everything I could find about Cambodia's recent history. That history came horribly to life the next day on our stop at the city's most infamous tourist attraction, security prison 21, or S-21. Renamed the Tuol Sleng Genocide Museum, this is a horrible, horrible place, as frightening and haunting as Auschwitz or Dachau.

Toward the end of the reign of the Khmer Rouge the sole purpose of S-21 was to extract confessions from political prisoners before they were executed. In 1978 and '79, as the regime's top leaders became increasingly paranoid, they began arresting even their most loyal supporters, blaming them for everything from poor crop yields to their military setbacks against a significantly more competent Vietnamese army. In a vicious cycle of madness, inmates were tortured until they gave up names, any names, and then these victims were brought in and tortured until *they* revealed names. Innocence or guilt was beside the point, since under torture prisoners would admit to whatever the interrogators asked for. Of the between 17,000 and 20,000 prisoners who entered S-21 between 1975 and 1979, there are seven known survivors.

Touring the museum today, even thirty years after the prison was liberated and quickly closed, is an unforgettable experience. Bloodstains are everywhere on the walls and floor. In some rooms instruments of torture are displayed. Pliers used to pull out teeth sit macabre-like next to toothless skulls. Other walls are plastered with photographs of the mutilated bodies of prisoners just as they were found by the Vietnamese, chained to their beds, murdered by their fleeing captors.

Especially haunting are the thousands of photographs of expressionless faces. The jailors must have taken a picture of every incoming inmate. Our guide told us that his entire family was tortured and killed at S-21. Every day he goes to work and imagines what his family went through. This young man offered this information matter of-factly, and I could not get it out of my mind that every day he relates the same information to new tourists. He tells them that instead of a set admission price, they can decide how much to donate. I shuddered, in a daze as I walked through the interrogation center with Virginia and Amanda. What could we possibly pay to compensate for such horror?

Prisoners at the notorious Khmer Rouge prison, S-21.

That afternoon we traveled a few hours out of town to an area known as the Killing Fields, where large numbers of people had been killed and buried by the Khmer Rouge. At a memorial, inside a glass-enclosed tower skulls were piled on top of tattered, bloodstained clothes. The day we visited, hundreds, maybe thousands, of butterflies were fluttering all over the field. The scene was eerie, like something out of a Fellini movie.

Virginia had had enough so she turned in while Amanda and I headed to the Patio Bar not far from the hotel. As two foreign women, we were concerned about our safety, but the concierge assured us we would be all right at this particular restaurant just off a main square.

We were seated on a second story balcony overlooking the street, and although we had a terrific view of the city, our location lent itself to people shouting up at us. We heard everything from "Hey lady, hey lady, throw me a dollar" to "I need your help," to, worst of all, "I have a baby, hey, take my baby."

I couldn't stop myself. I was obsessed with learning everything I could about life in Cambodia, and I started grilling our waitress. She had three small children at home, she told me, and she worked at the bar "so I don't end up in the red light."

Red light? I thought, before I realized she was talking about the red light district.

Amanda had begun talking with a Frenchman, or at least he said he was a French producer filming a movie in Phnom Penh. I didn't think to ask what kind of movie. All of a sudden she felt dizzy and a little nauseous, so I jumped up and said, "We need to get you back to the hotel!" I helped her downstairs and into a taxi, a three-wheeled automated rickshaw called a tuk-tuk, and we rushed the few blocks back to our hotel.

Amanda was sick in the lobby, and one of the staff suggested someone might have slipped something into her drink. For a moment I felt terrified. Kidnappings of young girls and human trafficking are huge problems in Southeast Asia and Amanda was tall, gorgeous, western, and eighteen years old.

Fortunately, by the time I got Amanda into bed she was already feeling better. But *I* couldn't sleep. My mind was racing. All I kept thinking about was how does a country function like this? Why were Cambodians living in such extreme poverty and hopelessness when neighboring countries like Vietnam and Thailand had vibrant economies that had begun to compete globally? Why was Cambodia falling through the cracks?

When my insomnia got the better of me I wandered down to the lobby. After a few minutes a girl came by on a motorbike. I don't know what possessed me, but I walked out to the street and asked if she would drive me to the red light district. I know it sounds insane, but it never occurred to me that this might be unsafe. I'm not normally a physically bold person, and certainly I'm not foolhardy, but I had to see this for myself.

At the outskirts of the red light district my driver refused to take me any further. She kept repeating, "It's not safe ma'am, it's not safe." I thought of Bill and of how he would not be happy with me at this moment, but I wanted to be able to visualize this part of Cambodia. I guess I was frightened at the thought that Srelin and her friends could end up here. I wanted to see it to make it real, perhaps as an incentive for me to do what I could to protect them.

The scene that spread out before my eyes was worse than I had imagined. Later I read that thirty percent of the prostitutes working in Phnom Penh's red light district are children, and that one in five tourists comes to Cambodia specifically to seek out prostitutes. I was so naïve that only gradually did it dawn on me that tourists routinely approach Srelin and the other girls working near the temples about buying something other than the trinkets they are selling.

I later learned much more about the sex trade that still exists in Cambodia by reading Somaly Mam's riveting memoir, *The Road of Lost Innocence*. This heroic woman was sold into sexual slavery by her grandfather when she was twelve years old and for the next decade was shuttled through different brothels, suffering unspeakable acts of brutality. A decade later she managed to escape, and somehow she found the strength and courage to become one of the world's leading activists fighting against human trafficking. Her book chronicles the stories of girls as young as six sold by their mothers to brothels in order to repay a debt, and of children being raped and beaten every day.

"In Siem Reap," she writes, "an ordinary girl, not a virgin, might bring up to fifteen dollars for about five days of work. Four girls will make you almost $1,500 a month, and cost you nothing but a bit of rice and a few guns."[2]

The book haunted me for months. At the time of my visit to the red light district I was ignorant of these horrors. Nonetheless, even on the fringe of this infamous, brutal place I could see girls as young as ten sitting on porches waiting for their next "trick"—a trick that might pay a dollar.

I returned to my hotel distraught, focused, and somehow changed. I felt for this country, or rather, I had a feeling that I wanted to do something to help. I *knew* something was going to happen; it had already happened to me. I was returning to Singapore with a lot to think about and a great deal to do.

---

2. *The Road of Lost Innocence* by Somaly Mam, Spiegel & Grau Trade Paperback Edition, 2009, page 157.

THREE

Finding the Orange

Back in Singapore a jumble of thoughts crowded my brain. No wonder I had a constant headache. Only one thing was certain: all my thoughts led back to the children I had met and to the villages and schools I had visited.

Especially the children. Their smiles, their patience, their openness to all my dumb questions, and particularly their simple, almost ethereal yearning to go to school had won me over. Despite their difficult lives and the backdrop of the genocide of their parents' generation, they seemed to have no guile.

But what could I do? Instead of sleeping, I constantly mulled over how to formalize some kind of program to help these girls and others like them get a proper education and have some hope for the future. Sure, I had sponsored a handful of them so they could go to school for a few months, but even I wasn't so naïve as to think that simply handing Samedi

$300 would change their lives in any meaningful way, much less have any kind of impact on a country's educational system.

I was wracked with a recurring thought: what could I do to help these girls and thousands like them make something of their lives? I had an overwhelming feeling that I had to do something, and that I *would* do something. It was like a fever, or a song you can't get out of your brain. But in this case it was a song with lyrics of my own making, telling me to *do something.*

But what exactly? Create orphanages like Christina Noble? Sponsor more children so they could go to school without having to scrounge for the money to pay for it? Somehow establish a way to pay teachers to teach? Build better, cleaner schools? They all sounded like good ideas but I had no clue where to begin. All these possibilities were racing inside me, and I was obsessed with grabbing hold and wrestling with every one of them.

After a few days in Singapore Virginia and Amanda flew home to Austin. As I drove them to the Singapore airport I couldn't stop talking about the things I wanted to do in Siem Reap.

I can't say Virginia ever completely understood what would develop into a full-grown passion on my part to build schools in Cambodia. After all, she was no bleeding heart. She had been one of the few members of her graduating class not to wear a gas mask while receiving her diploma from UC Berkeley during the infamous "Summer of Love." Nevertheless, she saw what I saw during those first forty-eight hours in Siem Reap, and it opened her eyes too as to how the other half lived.[3] Always upbeat when it came to my potential and what was possible for me to accomplish, that's exactly how she met my excitement about Cambodia. I knew

---

3. Actually, it's less than half, but it's still horrifying. According to the World Bank, 950 million people in developing countries live in extreme poverty, on less than $1.25 a day. That's about one in seven people on the planet.

it was a place where I could so some good, and as usual, she encouraged me to follow my heart.

Singapore

As soon as Virginia and Amanda returned to Texas I called my best friends in Singapore to ask for their help. Singapore is a city like no other, a unique blend of East and West. On the one hand, its infrastructure out-Wests the West in its modern design, six-star hotels, cosmopolitan restaurants, and mega casinos. A British colony for more than a hundred years, it is now an independent nation, the world's fourth leading financial center, and it plays a key role in international trade and finance in the region.

On the other hand, Singapore's Eastern culture imposes strict laws against jaywalking, littering, and chewing gum. It has a mandatory sentence of caning for vandalism offenses.

When I arrived home after that first visit to Cambodia, Bill and I had lived in Singapore for almost two years. Before that, we had lived in Los Angeles, and our final year there had been a difficult one for me. That's because Austin was twelve and a handful and Riley only four when Bronson was born in November of 2000 with a heart murmur, a broken shoulder, and the same condition Riley had had as an infant, craniosynostosis. It's when the bones in the back of an infant's head don't come together properly.

We had some scary times with Bronson, who wore a special helmet for the first few months of his life to relieve pressure on his brain and to make sure there was enough room in his skull to allow it to grow properly. A newborn grows so fast that twice a week for six months I made the three-hour round trip to Burbank with Bronson so his helmet could be adjusted. He is fine now, but with Bill out of town so frequently and with two other young children at home, my life had become centered around Riley's four-year-old demands, Austin's soccer games and school plays, and Bronson's frequent trips to the doctor and hospital.

Riley with Bill, 1998; Bronson with Bill's parents, 2000.

Finally, in early 2001 I told Bill I couldn't do this alone any longer. He had been traveling quite a bit, and after a stressful day with Bronson's pediatric cardiologist, who told me that our baby's heart murmur might be more serious than initially diagnosed, and a conversation with my ailing mother whose Alzheimer's was worsening daily, I felt overwhelmed.

Bill knew he had to make a choice between work and family, and he chose family, reluctantly resigning as head of NCR Corporation's retail and financial group, a job he loved and was very good at.

That's just one reason why I adore Bill. He's a tremendously hard worker, has flown millions of miles for work, and is a dedicated, brilliant leader. But providing for and being part of our family has always come first.

Then, out of nowhere, we received good news.

"You're not going to believe this," Bill said to me one day, "but I've just been offered a job with Dell that's going to allow us to move back to Austin."

This really was welcome news. I still had many friends in Austin and a community of support to help me through scary moments with Bronson. Just having Virginia to lean on would be a Godsend.

By the spring of 2001 I had found a house in Austin and had begun enrolling the kids in school for the following fall. Around the first week of May we were preparing to move when Bill came home and announced, "Change of plans. Dell needs me to go to Singapore as president of APJ (Asia-Pacific-Japan)."

What a blow this was, but I was determined to roll with it. After all I had been through with Bronson, there was no way Bill was going to start commuting halfway around the world. We'd *never* see him. Bill and I knew we had to be together as a family.

Bill asked me to try Singapore for a year, and although I was disappointed not to be moving back to Austin, I figured I could do anything for a year. I decided to look at it as an adventure, a vacation almost.

Although we stayed almost a decade, I never had reason to regret the decision to move to Singapore. About three-quarters of its 4.8 million people are ethnic Chinese, but the island also has a large foreign population, including about 100,000 U.S. expatriates. It has good schools, and English is the primary language. It is also an ideal hub for travelling anywhere in Asia, with a huge international airport as centrally located as one can be in the vast Asia-Pacific. Singapore is just off the southern tip of the Malay Peninsula, eighty-five miles north of the equator, about five hundred miles north of Indonesia.

The U.S. community in Singapore is tightknit and supportive. It's an interesting dynamic. No one exactly has relatives down the road, so pretty much everyone is in the same situation. Instantly you are a member of the community just by virtue of being there, and the transient nature of everyone's lives makes people open to making new friends. Since the average stay in Singapore for expats is two years, you need to get to know people quickly. Your friends are probably about to move away, so you have to be open to making new ones.

Singapore does take some getting used to. One of my biggest challenges was remembering to drive on the left side of the road. For the first six months I constantly played a little game with myself, reminding myself aloud, "Righty righty, lefty lefty" so I wouldn't suddenly find myself driving headlong into traffic.

Compared to the United States, even Los Angeles, everything feels tight and close together in Singapore. It is a tiny island, after all, smaller than Manhattan. Another big difference is that because wages are so low, expats tend to have a lot of help in the form of drivers, nannies, and cooks. That frees up spouses who are there because their husbands or wives (mostly husbands, even in the twenty-first century) are working for a multinational in the region. For me, this meant I had a coterie of dedicated volunteers at my fingertips once Caring for Cambodia got started.

In the Genes

By the time I visited Siem Reap for the first time I had made some good friends within Singapore's expat community. Upon my return, I turned to them for help. I didn't want my trip to Cambodia to become a memory of a vacation that fit neatly into a photo album. Bill was out of town, but all of a sudden I shifted into high gear, while at the same time settling back into my Singapore routine as the mom of an infant, a first-grader, and a high schooler.

First, I invited a few people over for wine to talk about what I had just experienced. Many of them, including Jade Ausley, Marybeth Shay, and Carolyn Edds, are still involved with CFC. I tried to communicate my passion, which wasn't difficult since the level of enthusiasm I had felt standing in the schoolyard in Siem Reap had not really ebbed.

"We cannot allow this to happen at our doorstep," I told them. "It's not okay for people to live like this, with children unable to go to school because they can't afford $5 a month."

Somehow these women understood. Carolyn had been to Siem Reap, so she knew firsthand what I was talking about. But even those who had not yet been there rallied around the idea of doing something. From the start, I knew the "something" would be related to education, but it took a while for me to realize this pull was in my genes.

I was born Jamie Hickey in Biloxi, Mississippi. I grew up in Schertz, Texas, a small town outside San Antonio, not far from Randolph Air Force Base, in archetypical Texas country. This meant horses, cattle, and football. Add to all this a dash of military and you have Schertz in the 1970s and '80s.

My mother was a war bride. She came over on the *Queen Mary* from England after marrying her first husband, an American GI with whom she had three kids, my brother Rudy and my sisters Cori and Valorie. They were later divorced. (After CFC was born, Valorie's frequent visits to Singapore to help take care of my kids while I was in Siem Reap meant the world to me.) My mother's twenty-five-year marriage to my father until he passed away in 1983 produced my older sister Veronica and me.

My father grew up in Chicago but went to officer's training school in Dallas. He must have liked Texas because by the time I came along he had retired at the age of forty-two after more than twenty years in the Air Force, and he and my mom had settled in Schertz.

As far as I was concerned, I got a raw deal. My sisters and brother were Air Force brats, moving from place to place, so while Veronica had her prom in Paris, mine was in New Braunfels, just up the highway from Schertz. I never had a passport until I married Bill.

My family. Mom and Dad when they were young. My sister, Veronica, and mom at my wedding. Everyone—from oldest to me—Valorie, her husband, Bob, and their daughter Natalie, Rudy, Cori and Veronica, my mom holding me, and Dad holding the cat. Me at the age of three. One of my favorite photos of Mom and Dad.

My dad retired from the Air Force to work with kids. Hired as the principal of St. Monica's Catholic School in Converse, just a few miles south of Schertz, he held the position for ten years, until the day he died.

My mom picked up the education bug too. After earning her teaching certificate, she became a preschool and kindergarten aide at St. Monica's. That was pretty impressive considering she came from an extremely poor English coal miner's family and had only gone to school through the sixth grade. My sister Veronica also became a teacher.

I don't think I recognized the direct line from my father's love of education and my involvement with CFC until my mother passed away in 2004. In delivering the eulogy for my mom, the priest from St. Monica's Church also talked a lot about my dad. I was only seventeen when he died, and I had forgotten what an inspirational educator he was and how so many people looked up to him. He loved what he did and the kids loved him. He was always *that guy*, a "We're going to catch a ride with Mr. Hickey" sort of a person.

The Beginnings of CFC

Developing a long-term plan for making a significant contribution in Siem Reap was going to take some time, but my friends in Singapore and I wanted to come up with something we could do to impact the schools immediately. I knew that my most important task at this early stage was to convince Samedi and the dozen or so girls I was sponsoring, as well as their parents, the teachers, and the school administrators, that I was serious and that I wasn't going to disappear after promising to make a difference.

I wanted to make a statement that would show we were committed, that we could be counted on to fulfill our promises. I did not want them to think I was just another Westerner who vowed to stay in touch but then disappeared. I was intent on returning to Siem Reap the following weekend with tangible evidence of my commitment. I knew this was going to be the start of something powerful.

As a group, the other women and I decided that our first area of concentration would be assembling donated school supplies for shipment to Siem Reap. I think it was Jade who suggested putting them in backpacks as a way to package the materials we thought we could accumulate. Improving the schools and figuring out a way to pay the teachers were more daunting challenges, but sending care packages with the things I had noticed missing during my first visit was something we could do immediately.

Within a week my house had become a warehouse of backpacks and school supplies. A few phone calls multiplied our core group of volunteers, with friends urging their friends to call their friends. Suddenly piles of toothbrushes, t-shirts, pencils, and notebooks were spilling out of my spare room into the hall and living room. After we sent out an email asking for certain pieces of clothing we were also flooded with flip-flops, shirts, and shorts.

In essence I became the Salvation Army in Singapore, and my friends and I worked hard to put out the word: "If you have things you don't need, bring them to Jamie and she'll take them to Cambodia."

We organized all the clothes by sizes and created an assembly line to fill the backpacks. In each boys' backpack we put a baseball cap; in each girls', a barrette. Every nook and cranny in our spare room and den was filled with boxes.

The situation has since changed, but at the time Singapore, like the rest of Asia, lacked a strong culture of giving. Nonprofit organizations were not an important part of society, yet within the expatriate community I think there was a latent hunger to give back some of what we had received. We were living in paradise and we knew it, while just a few hours away children were in need. We were inspired. We were committed. We were changed.

We made a number of missteps, of course. We started out with a lot of donated sneakers, but we soon realized that the mud that clings to everything during Cambodia's monsoon season made sneakers impractical. Someone even dropped off golf clubs, and although the kids we were trying to help had never even heard of golf, I took them anyway. If I couldn't find a use for an item in Cambodia, I found a charity in Singapore that could.

Another notch on the learning curve was a flirtation with trying to initiate a "sponsor a child" fundraising campaign. Early on I frequently looked to see if we could emulate some of what other organizations were doing to raise funds, and I was intrigued with sponsor-a-child programs. We worked hard to give it a try, particularly Jill Kirwin, the volunteer who ran the program for us. We took pictures of dozens of children, writing their names and a little caption under each one, then bound these pictures in a book and took them to meetings to try to encourage people to sponsor a particular child.

Creepily, this reminded me of the photos of kids at the S-21 prison standing against the wall holding a piece of paper with their name on it. A bigger problem was that the program was impossible to administer. After collecting a small amount of money, we had to find the family, give them the donation, and then constantly make sure the funds were being used properly. We were knee deep into it before I had to backpedal. Other organizations must have had a hundred people working to administer this one program, I realized.

The backpack drive had none of these problems, and to my delight it was a natural way to get my own children involved. I was really passionate about the idea that Bronson, Riley, and Austin, who were definitely living a privileged life, needed to see what was going on elsewhere on this earth we all shared.

Bill and I have always tried to make giving back part of our lives. The children have heard Bill say a thousand times, "To whom much is given, much is expected," and I felt responsible for making certain they saw that mantra in action. Usually our efforts were small ones, like when I led a campaign to put seat belts in school buses while living in North Carolina, or when I volunteered at a school for the deaf, or took cookies to the children at Brackenridge Hospital back home in Austin.

Before moving to Singapore I had also been active in a nonprofit organization in Los Angeles called Vistas for Children. It raises money for charitable organizations that help needy local children find food, shelter, and healthcare, and "adopts" individual families in need. I had helped found Junior Vistas, which gave the children of volunteers at Vistas for Children the opportunity to get involved as well. It was exciting to see young people and not just their moms and dads working to raise awareness about the lives of their less fortunate neighbors and participating in hands-on activities like wrapping holiday gifts and visiting children at area hospitals.

But after a while, I became pretty burned out by all the fundraising. That's not how I felt I could best give back. I enjoyed the pizza parties with the kids much more than I did the gala ballroom events. I wanted to get my hands dirty, not dress up and raise money. Bill, too, was ready for us to do something else; he has never been a big fan of tuxedos.

Consequently, as I thought about what to do in Siem Reap, I knew it had to involve our own children and that it had to touch the children of Siem Reap in a meaningful way.

Cambodia was all I could think about. As I talked to Carolyn and Jade and the others about what we were going to do in Siem Reap, I kept visualizing a place where people living in villages right near one of the most beautiful temples on earth had no food or clean water, and where naked children and families lived in filth. I could not get those images out of my mind, or completely lose the smell of them. I wanted to bring my kids with me on the next plane and plop them down in a village and tell them, "Look around. What do you see? What do you *really* see?"

On my first few visits to Siem Reap in 2003 I took countless photos. I didn't yet own a digital camera, so I used a twenty-four-hour photography service in Singapore. Jade and I spent many moments together in the car outside the store waiting for the photographs to be ready. I think we helped keep one family in business.

I constantly showed the photos to Bill and the kids, trying to explain what Siem Reap was like and that our family was going to do something to change it. I was jazzed about getting my kids involved, and pointed out to them the photographs of the girls I had met and the schools I wanted to improve. Talking it all through with my kids, telling them they would go to Siem Reap to see for themselves why I was so excited, somehow became part of the promise I vowed to keep.

Our three boys, ages fourteen, six, and two, definitely thought I was nuts, but even two-year-old Bronson could see that I was serious. From the moment my life was turned upside down by my first visit to Cambodia, my fixation over the disparity between life in Siem Reap and life in Singapore had a lot to do with the lives of *our* children compared to the lives of the girls I had met.

Meanwhile, I didn't want any time to pass before my return to Cambodia. Kaye Bach, who would soon become such a crucial part of CFC's success, liked to tease me by calling me a lawnmower because I would never allow grass to grow beneath my feet. Ten days after I returned from my first trip I flew back to Siem Reap, basically retracing my steps of the previous weekend.

Again Samedi took me to the temples and roadside stands, where the same young girls were selling souvenirs and other trinkets. I had many questions for them, mostly repeats of what I had already asked. "How do you live? How long have you worked like this? What do your parents do?" "How often do you go to school?" "What do you want to be when you grow up?"

This last question tended to stump them. At best they would mention becoming a tour guide or a tuk-tuk driver. They didn't seem to really understand the question, and I finally realized this was because they had little idea of hope or success or what a better life might look like. They had no concept of what it meant to dream about a better future. They were very much in the now, and their now was centered around earning a few dollars selling souvenirs in order to help feed their families and to go to school.

Back in Singapore I resumed working with what was now a core group of committed expats. I kept in touch with Samedi by phone and also sent him information by email, which he could pick up at one of the Internet cafes that had begun to dot downtown Siem Reap, although at this time they usually consisted of just a bar with a lone computer. I was always asking him about the girls I had sponsored and how many backpacks we would need.

When the backpacks were filled and ready to go, a few of us went down to Chinatown and for $10 apiece bought twenty huge duffel bags. Although the girls I had met attended different schools, we decided to distribute all twenty duffels, stuffed with the backpacks, at Kravaan, the first school I had visited.

Everything began snowballing quickly. During this same time, we were trying to come up with a name for our fledgling organization, and we soon settled on Caring for Cambodia (CFC). That seemed to say what we were thinking. Our colors were white and bright orange, like the robes of the Buddhist monks, which to me symbolized hope and possibility.

We could see this was going to take a lot of work, whatever "this" turned out to be, but we were confident that we were ready for the challenge. I knew in my heart that we would make a difference. I felt like I could see forward, and it was always a good feeling to know I had Bill behind me one hundred percent. I talked to him constantly about what I was doing and the next steps I wanted to take.

On my third or fourth trip to Siem Reap Marybeth, Jade, Carolyn, and I visited the school in Kravaan to distribute the backpacks. Samedi had paved the way by letting the principal and teachers know we'd be arriving.

The kids lined up in rows in front of the building and we started to hand out a backpack to each child. They were excited and it was wonderful, but with a couple of rows left we started to run out. Suddenly I wondered if we had brought enough, and I held my breath as we reached the last row. What if one or two kids were left without a backpack and had to watch every other child happily unveil their new t-shirt and supplies?

I needn't have worried, because our first orange moment was about to occur: the very last child in the very last row was given the very last backpack. Someone was watching over us.

The backpacks with all the goodies inside became a signature welcome to CFC students and a continuing source of excitement and pride for them. Filling them became a full-time job for one our hardest-working volunteers, Christy Miller.

CFC students receiving backpacks at the Bakong School opening, 2004.

We used to tease Christy about walking into a school in Siem Reap wearing her Chanel hat and Gucci glasses ("Jeez," we'd say, "she looks good even in the dirt!"), but our words were full of affection. Christy, also from Austin and married to David, who worked for Dell before following Bill to Lenovo, was orange from the moment she landed in Cambodia. She never had a problem rolling up her sleeves and getting her hands dirty. She participated in the first Make a Difference (MAD) trip in 2004, and in Singapore she took charge of organizing our goods donations. She singlehandedly created order out of the chaos of people constantly giving us all sorts of supplies to put in the backpacks.

Christy was so organized. If someone dropped off ten shirts consisting of two mediums and eight smalls, she immediately wrote the information in a file so we always knew precisely what we had on hand. She'd get the duffel bags organized, prepped, and ready to go, and find someone going to Siem Reap who could deliver them. Sometimes on our trips to Siem Reap my family and I would take with us a dozen huge duffel bags filled with supplies. We'd beg the reservationists not to charge us for extra baggage, explaining that it was all for charity, and usually they were nice about it.

Between my initial visit in late January of 2003 and the first of May three months later, I returned to Siem Reap four or five times, always with the same pattern. Samedi would be my tour guide, and when he asked where I wanted to go, I'd say, "Let's drop by the school." Once there, I'd always want to know, "Where are the kids I sponsored? Did you buy the supplies with the money I left you?" Remarkably, the children were at school and the supplies were being used. Already progress was visible.

Not every experience was pleasant, but they all contributed to my determination to help create an educational system that would teach the younger generation a better way. One of these early 2003 visits coincided with Visakha Bucha, one of the most important days in Buddhism. Visakha Bucha commemorates three important incidents in the life of Buddha—the birth, the enlightenment, and the passing, all of which according to Buddhism occurred on the same date, during the Vesak full moon. On this day each year Buddhists throughout the world gather to worship the wisdom, purity, and compassion of the Buddha. In Siem Reap the Visakha Bucha celebration is a monumental event, with thousands of orange, burgundy, and yellow-robed monks gathering from all over Asia.

I found myself in the middle of a tremendous crowd, with a mother suddenly thrusting her infant at me. I couldn't understand her words but her intent was clear: she wanted me to take her baby.

The infant's eyes were open but she seemed to be unconscious, her expression dull and listless. I learned later that mothers force their babies to sniff glue in order to make their begging more effective.

The mother kept pushing her daughter at me. The baby's hand fell on mine and seemed to stay there. I kept saying, "No, I can't take your baby," while the mother begged, "Please! Please!" in English. I had seen this mother at the market using her baby to beg for money, but I was still flabbergasted and a little frightened.

Jade Ausley was with me that day and took a picture of the baby's hand laid over mine, a picture that we continue to use in our CFC materials as a symbol of our commitment, and a reminder that it is all about the children. That's a moment in time I will never forget, nor am I allowed to forget. For the duration of our decade in Asia I watched that mother and her child. At age eight, the little girl still couldn't walk and clearly had other serious health problems, no doubt related to sniffing glue as an infant.

This incident made me more determined than ever to understand Cambodia. During my next few visits my nights were mostly spent alone in my hotel room, poring through every book I could get my hands on to learn more about modern Cambodia and what the Cambodians, including Samedi, had gone through under the Khmer Rouge. During the day I peppered Samedi with more questions, or perhaps just the same questions phrased in a different way. I was talking fast, wanting to do so much so quickly that he must have thought I was pretty nutty, but he patiently guided me during those early days. We spent a lot of time together, and while he didn't talk much, I asked a lot of questions and he always answered the best he could.

I remember my third visit, sitting in the hotel lobby with Samedi holding several hundred more dollars, saying I wanted to keep sponsoring the girls and that I wanted him to buy school supplies for Kravaan. I was trying desperately to figure out how I could make what we were doing official, how we could build schools and pay good teachers and create meaningful change.

Samedi's demeanor never changed; he was always calm and thoughtful. Each time I left Siem Reap he would take the money and either by email or our increasingly frequent phone calls keep me informed about what he had done with it. But finally he told me he was in over his head.

Ung Savy, an Angel

I had been asking Samedi what it would take to sponsor a school, how to arrange a meeting with the appropriate government officials, and how to set up a system whereby CFC could pay the teachers even when the government did not.

Samedi was a talented and successful tour guide, and had done a terrific job of accurately and honestly dispensing the school supplies and the modest amounts of cash I had given him. But now he confessed that he did not know how to do what I was asking and that he was not the right person to take on the daunting task I was trying to foist upon him. This reality became clear to both of us, and I will always appreciate his honesty.

The fact is, I was in over my head too. We needed someone who could not only oversee the distribution of the funds and materials we were collecting, but also work with Siem Reap's educational system, including the Ministry of Education, to make certain our contributions would be welcomed and effective. This was a giant task, and I wasn't at all certain it would be easy to find someone with the wherewithal to pull it off. I began pressing Samedi to tell me if he knew anyone who could help me do what I was envisioning, and right away he had an idea.

At the same time he was giving me his recommendation, I sent an email to those in our Singapore group who had been to Cambodia, asking them if they had met anyone in Siem Reap who might be able to take charge of what we were trying to accomplish. One of our volunteers, Lisa McMullen, emailed back that she had met a tour guide who had really impressed her who also worked at one of the schools. Remarkably and almost simultaneously, Samedi and Lisa were recommending the same person!

This kind of thing happened so often during CFC's formative years that I almost started to take it for granted. Call it serendipity, or the blessings of a higher power, or just dumb good luck, but good things often fell into our laps. We started calling them "orange moments." The young man named Ung Savy, known as Savy (pronounced *sahfee*), was the best one of all.

The following week I met him, a slight man with a boyish face but a seriousness to his quick smile. Savy explained to me in English that he was a tour guide at the temples and a part-time English teacher at the elementary school in the small village of Spien Chrieve, as well as a full-time proponent of improving conditions there. I tried to convey to him how taken I was with his country and that I really wanted to help the children through education.

"I know you have heard this before," I told him, "but I've never been more serious about anything in my life. I don't really know how to do it, and I certainly can't do it myself, but I'm not giving up until I have put into place a way we can help children get a quality education. If you can help me, great; if not, maybe you can help me find someone who can."

I no doubt was speaking way too quickly for Savy to truly understand me. His English has since improved significantly, but the first time I met him I had difficulty understanding him. In any language he must have thought I was a little bit off my rocker, but he took the job without hesitation. At least I think he understood that I was offering him a job. There was no written agreement. We barely had a verbal understanding. Neither of us even tried to imagine what was in store for CFC; we both just took a leap of faith.

If I couldn't understand Savy very well, he later told me he could barely understand me at all. Who was this woman going on and on about helping children get an education, building schools, and changing his world? Nonetheless, he must have gotten the gist of it, for he realized I wanted him to be the person on the ground to turn an evolving dream into reality.

Once Savy signed on things really began to come together in a more official way; actually, in every way. Without knowing very much about each other, we had to trust one another profoundly. In a very short time Savy would have a lot of money in his hands, more money and more responsibility than he could possibly have imagined.

I saw something in Savy, just like I had seen something in those young girls I had met on my first few visits. I never wanted to let him down, and as we got going I didn't want to let the children, their parents, or their teachers down. That more than anything else is what drove me, and in the coming months and years it would spur me on during the many private moments when I questioned what in the world I was doing.

Mother's Day

In May of 2003 Bill and I traveled to Cambodia with our friends Jade and Greg Ausley. We arrived the week of Mother's Day and followed my typical routine, this time with Savy as our guide.

This was the first time Bill had been to Cambodia, so we visited the temples because I knew he would be wowed by Angor Wat and Angor Tom, and I was right. We also stopped at the village so Bill could meet the girls I had sponsored.

Along the way he saw exactly what I had seen—the unsanitary conditions, the mud-floored schools, the magnificent temples, the lines of people waiting to get into the hospital, and most of all, the beautiful children. I really didn't have to say anything to him. He had lived with my enthusiasm for months, and now he finally had the chance to see it for himself.

I was relieved but not surprised when we walked around the temples together and he shared my sense of being overtaken by an outside force. He kept saying to me, "I feel it, I feel it."

I don't know if Bill would have had the same commitment had it not been for the temples. As an engineer and a religious person, he was in awe of the miracle of them, that they still stood after all these centuries, that they were real, that they were something we could touch, and that at the same time they could touch us. Maybe God was speaking to us or maybe not, but sitting on a rock at one of the temples we felt struck by a lightning bolt of emotion telling us to do something more.

The next day I took Bill to the Kravaan School, the first school I had visited. One of the girls I had sponsored was sitting in the classroom next to the window with a piece of paper fastened with a safety pin to her blouse that read in English, "Sponsored by Jamie Amelio." There was my name, right on her heart. She'd had no idea I was coming to school that day, and I never saw anything like that again. Plain and simple, it felt like a signpost aimed directly at Bill and me.

Bill and I took a short walk past the school. I turned to him and said, "I think you know this has already changed my life. I'm different now. I have something to ask you."

I took a deep breath and continued. "It's Mother's Day, and I'd like to ask for a Mother's Day present. If you will build me a school here in Siem Reap, I swear to you, I will never ask you for another piece of jewelry. I am done with presents, I promise you. Just build me a school. It means the world to me."

"Jamie, are you serious?"

"I'm serious. I'm asking you right now."

I told him a school would cost $30,000 to build and that we needed $2,000 to get started. Today.

"You want me to hand over $2,000 to someone I don't know in a country as corrupt as Cambodia and just trust them to do what they say?"

"Pretty much, yes," I told him.

Bill and I have felt a unique connection since the day we met, on my twenty-eighth birthday. After a few dates we knew we were meant for each other. We eloped on New Year's Eve six weeks after we met, and in April had our fairytale wedding with Austin walking me down the aisle. Nine years later, halfway around the world, I was asking him to make another leap of faith, this time in both Savy and me.

I knew Bill was impressed by Savy's commitment to his country, but as a businessman he also wondered about Savy's lack of management experience. We spent a lot of time talking about it, because quite frankly, this was a tough decision. Savy was a tour guide making his way through life in Cambodia. Was he really prepared to take on this huge responsibility, one that could become larger and more complex than even we could anticipate?

We debated about several other people we had met, but I was convinced Savy was our guy. Bill agreed, despite his concern that this was a developing country pretty high up on the corruption list, where the best laid plans often don't work out.

"Look," I told him, "you figured out how to run a global company. I'm sure you can figure this out!"

It was an extremely emotional moment when Bill said, with tears in his eyes, "Okay, let's do it."

We would have to build trust very, very quickly, but CFC was about to build a school.

FOUR

Building a School

Savy looked confused when Bill and I handed him a check for $2,000. At first we thought he was surprised at the amount, or that he was concerned that we were asking him to sign a receipt, or that even after all my promises and return trips to Siem Reap since my first visit in January, he doubted my intentions to build schools and improve Cambodian education.

It did not occur to Bill or to me that Savy had never seen a check before, not to mention the inside of a bank, or that he had no idea what to do with what he later told us he considered a very expensive piece of paper.

"What is this?" he asked us.

"It's a check. A bank will give you money for it to start building a new school."

"*WHAT? Build a new school?*"

We told him that we knew people promised to build schools and never returned, but that we were different.

"We can do it," he said quietly.

We too thought we could do it, even as we sensed what Savy did not tell us until years later—that he felt overcome with honor and pride, but also nervousness at the trust we were placing in him. Perhaps it was just blind faith, or even blinder hope, but for some reason Bill and I believed Savy was going to be able to handle the challenge, that he was going to get the required permissions from the local government and Cambodia's Ministry of Education and find a contractor who could build a school for $30,000, using the $2,000 as a down payment.

We believed all this despite the fact that we knew Savy had never undertaken anything remotely like this before. He had never pretended otherwise. But somehow all three of us were convinced that his eagerness, optimism, and obvious competence would overcome his overwhelming inexperience. Since then I've often wondered if CFC would have succeeded without Savy.

At the time, there were only two banks in all of Siem Reap[4] and it was impossible to open a non-governmental organization (NGO) in either one of them. The next morning Savy walked into the Siem Reap Bank and used our check to open a bank account in his own name, the first one he had ever had.

The trust we had for each other went both ways. Savy knew perfectly well that building a new school would cost more than $2,000. He could get construction started, but what if Jamie and Bill Amelio disappeared?

---

4. Today there are more than a dozen banks in Siem Reap, most with ATM machines.

What if he never saw any more money? Savy told me years later how nervous he was once construction began, waiting for the next installment to be wired into his account. He paid daily visits to the bank, and the first few times money arrived I think he was a little amazed, and definitely relieved.

Ung Savy's Story

As I mentioned earlier, everyone in Cambodia past a certain age has a story, usually a horrible, unimaginable story, about their lives during the years when the Khmer Rouge was in power.

Savy was no exception, although I did not learn the full depth of his personal history until much later, when he made his first trip to Singapore to make a presentation before CFC's board of directors. Before then, his tortured past always seemed purposely hidden by his kind eyes, warm spirit, and remarkable, paradoxical optimism. A few times I'd heard him describe these years as "a living hell," but beyond that he never seemed to want to go and I never asked. Or maybe we were just too busy building schools.

Eventually I learned that Savy was born in 1969, the year the United States Air Force began carpet-bombing eastern Cambodia, drawing Cambodia headlong into the Vietnam War. The Nixon Administration insisted the bombing was directed against legitimate Vietnamese and Khmer Rouge targets, but the half million tons of bombs ended up killing at least 100,000 Cambodian civilians.

In April of 1970 American and South Vietnamese forces crossed into Cambodia, sparking massive protests across the United States. President Nixon soon withdrew American troops from Cambodia, but the U.S. bombings continued until August of 1973.

As Savy told us at the board meeting, "Until the age of six I was living in war. Kids at this age need nurturing, love, caring, healthy food, good advice, and parental oversight. They are blank slates, eager to learn and grow. But for me, I had no chance at any of these things. What my brain recorded was killing—lots of killing, fighting, and hate."

At seven, Savy was forced to live separately from his parents in a work camp with other children. Under the Khmer Rouge, every child was put to work. Savy's job was to destroy termite mounds, clear the brush, and mix it with human waste into fertilizer. He'd have to taste it to make sure it was ready, then spread the concoction through the rice paddies. He worked twelve to fifteen hours each day seven days a week for four years, perpetually scrounging for food and sleeping on wooden slats next to dozens of other children.

"I learned a lot of lessons during these years," Savy told us. "Most of all I learned to strongly hate and to accept the killing of others as part of our daily lives. They made us work so hard and they taught us to hate our parents and even kill our parents."

Over the years Savy has told me about some of his close calls, including how his grandfather jumped on top of him when he was a young child to protect him when bombs began falling all around them. Another time Savy leapt out of his hammock just before it was blown to smithereens. He also spent days lying alone in the woods with a fever after being bitten by a spider.

During the first few years of his life his family was constantly on the move, either forced by the Khmer Rouge or to escape constant bombings. On more than one occasion his family home burned to the ground and he watched neighbors die in the blaze as he fled into the jungle.

In 1979 the Vietnamese Army marched into Cambodia and forced the Khmer Rouge out of power, ending four years of mass killings, forced labor, and widespread terror. Savy was ten, and with the Vietnamese in control, he bounced from place to place, eventually attending school for the first time at the age of thirteen. After finishing the sixth grade, he was conscripted into the Vietnamese Army.

He told me, "My education as a soldier taught me to defend my country and community from enemy invaders, and this time, how to kill the enemy."

The army also gave him the opportunity to learn English. Because it was against the law in Cambodia to study any foreign language except Vietnamese and Russian, Savy studied surreptitiously at night with other likeminded soldiers.

Savy says that sometime in 1990 he began hearing rumors that the United Nations was planning to enter the country to set up what would be the first democratic Cambodian elections. He had only the vaguest notion of what the United Nations was, or even what an election was. "I basically just understood that foreigners were coming to Cambodia to do something that was supposed to be a good thing for our country and for our people," he told us.

In 1993, the same year Savy was discharged from the army, international U.N. armed forces did arrive in Cambodia to coordinate the election. With the U.N. presence, life in this Southeast Asian country that had lost a quarter of its population to starvation and genocide finally became more open and free.

Savy took advantage of the change by returning to school and by doing everything he could to improve his English. Whenever he saw U.N. troops in town or in the market he went out of his way to translate for them. Soon he was spending most of his time with U.N. personnel and soldiers. "I ate with them, slept in their camp, and became their friend," he remembers.

Several of the U.N. soldiers encouraged Savy to move to Siem Reap, where they thought he had a better chance of using his constantly improving English skills to find employment as a tour guide. But work there was hard to find. He began volunteering at the elementary school in Spien Chrieve, teaching English, and for several months he slept on a hammock on the school grounds. When some of the children's parents started occasionally paying him a little something, he was able to rent a motorbike from one of the families and use it to take tourists to the temples. He also found some work as a tuk-tuk driver. In 1998 he was accepted into a six-week tour guide training course sponsored by the Cambodian government, and upon graduation was certified as an official guide at Angor Wat and Angor Tom. All the while, almost unbeknownst to him, he was making contacts within the Siem Reap community that would prove invaluable to us both.

By the time I met him, things were looking up for Savy. Given the long and torturous path that led him to me, or me to him, no wonder he was undaunted by the relatively easy task of wading through Cambodia's bureaucracy in order to build a school and keep it running.

Our First School

After Savy successfully opened a bank account, our next step was to decide where to build our first school. Savy suggested Spien Chrieve, the village where he had been volunteering as an English teacher. The only school there was an extremely dilapidated one-room structure in one of the poorest villages in the area, located about twenty minutes from the temples by mostly dirty roads, far removed from tourists or any industry related to tourism. I was intrigued, so on my next visit to Siem Reap Savy took me to see the village.

The road leading into Spien Chrieve parallels the Siem Reap River. Because of the annual flooding during monsoon season, the bamboo-thatched houses sit on stilts high above the ground. Most of them are open, without walls. Chickens, oxen, and stray dogs congregate in the shade under the raised floors, causing their stink to permeate the homes. As I drove through Spien Chrieve for the first time I could see naked children running everywhere, playing in the mud, and washing themselves in the river, which tripled as bathwater, latrine, and a source of drinking water.

The school was just as unsanitary. One building was really just an open-air hut, slightly raised from the ground with wooden planks for flooring. Classes were conducted in the adjacent cement building that was more like a cement box with dirt flooring and open-air windows. Savy told me that 260 kids attended school in that blindingly dusty (or muddy when it rained) small space.

I did not need much convincing that this was a good place to start, but now that we knew where to build, it was up to Savy to figure out how. The government of Cambodia is a parliamentary democratic monarchy with a prime minister as the head of government within a multi-party system. Legislative power rests in the two chambers of parliament, the National Assembly and the Senate. In reality, however, decision-making is very localized, centered on each community's *chau sangkart*, or community leader. Savy's first move was to pay a visit to the *chau sangkart* in Spien Chrieve.

"There's this American woman who keeps visiting from Singapore," Savy told him. "She says she wants to build a new school. She's given me the money to do it. Can we build a new building where the school is now?"

With an easy nod, the *chau sangkart* suggested Savy run the idea by other village leaders, and Savy found no opposition. We weren't asking for anything except to build on the existing site, so the community had no reason to oppose our plan.

Savy then had a similar conversation with Siem Reap's Minister of Education. Given all that we had heard about government corruption, it was remarkable that we never had to pay anyone under the table. I attribute that to Savy's presentation, and to his continual advice to be discreet about what we were doing. We weren't trying to operate or start a new school or to subvert local authority. We were only offering to construct a new building and support the current teachers and administrators in any way we could. The Ministry of Education would still be in charge; we were just constructing a new building.

With the approvals in hand, Savy now had to find someone with the wherewithal to build a small schoolhouse. Not surprisingly, he knew the perfect person, a Mr. San who was building schools throughout Cambodia. As for me, I was beginning to think Savy knew everyone in this part of the country.

Mr. San's family's story was different from almost everyone else I met in Cambodia. Most former Khmer Rouge members vehemently deny their involvement, or at least their culpability. If that is impossible, they are typically ostracized to the outskirts of the community. While former members of the Khmer Rouge currently hold high positions in the national government, at the local level there is an unspoken message of "I know what you did in the war" directed at them from many villagers.

Mr. San's family fit none of these patterns. Both his parents had served in the Khmer Rouge army. San himself was a nurse during the Pol Pot era, and his father became the *chau sangkart* in Bakong, a village not far from Spien Chrieve. Nevertheless, the San family remained popular and respected. This was an anomaly during the post-Pol Pot years, but the Sans had treated people fairly and always supported both the Buddhist monastery and the local schools.

Mr. San agreed to build us a school in Spien Chrieve for $30,000 using an architectural design created by the World Bank for building attractive, efficient, economical schoolhouses in developing countries.

Savy was showing us that he was a miracle worker, something I would come to expect as I got to know him better. Within three months, all was in place: he had the money (from Bill and me), the approvals (from the *chau sangkart* and the local Ministry of Education), the contractor (Mr. San), and the design (from the World Bank). In June, construction began.

Throughout the summer and fall of 2003 I continued to shuttle back and forth every few weeks to Siem Reap from Singapore, often taking a different Amelio child with me so that each one would feel involved in our family's endeavor. I was also in almost daily contact with Savy either by phone or email. I could have made a flipbook of the photographs he regularly emailed me showing the progress of the construction. It was truly amazing to see, like an out-of-focus mirage transforming into something real.

The rise of the new school became a seminal event in the post Khmer Rouge history of Spien Chrieve. News that this building, this beautiful new building, was going to be their school spread throughout the village, and people of all ages started showing up at the construction site to watch.

In addition to constructing a new building we also renovated the existing structure, shoring up its foundation, reconstructing the walls, putting in real windows and doors, and painting it inside and out. The renovated building would become the school library and eventually the computer room and a kindergarten.

Back in Singapore I organized a group of teachers at the Singapore American School (SAS) that Bronson, Riley, and Austin attended, as well as a few expat friends with teaching experience, into an informal advisory group that we began to call our Education Committee. It was headed by Annie Meyer Stowell, an educator from California and one of the nicest, bubbliest people you'll ever meet. A life-size living Glenda, the Good Witch in the *Wizard of Oz*, Annie's halo is especially bright. She can quiet down a room of rowdy kids with just a sidelong look, then enchant them with a few words. She has an adopted daughter from Cambodia and one from China, and her heart was immediately into what were trying to do with CFC.

Annie asked me how the new committee could be most helpful and I responded with a question of my own. "If you had hardly any money and you wanted to do one thing in your classroom that would have a powerful impact, what would it be?"

The committee's overwhelming response was, "Make the classroom a happy place."

That seemed like a simple enough suggestion. Anyone who knows me knows I love color in my house. I thought, "Well, good, we'll paint the classrooms."

I presented the idea to Savy, not knowing I was crossing some sort of strict cultural line. For some reason, in Cambodia in 2003 painting the exterior of school buildings white or yellow was common enough, but no one had ever considered painting interior walls anything other than white. It was like I was suggesting putting doors on the ceiling.

"Please, just trust me," I said to Savy. "Let's paint one room and see what happens."

We ended up painting the library a luscious green, and people were immediately enraptured. We also had the school's most talented art student, Pen Rithy, paint a magnificent animal mural. Later he created something similar in the other classrooms, often assisted by our CFC volunteers.

At the school's grand opening villagers broke into huge smiles when they saw the different colored rooms. Even the government officials, who usually did their best not to smile, nodded their heads and murmured, "H-m-m, well, okay . . ."

A simple thing like adding a couple of coats of paint had such a buoyant effect on the teachers and students that painting is now our first priority every time we take over a school. Today, the walls of our classrooms, libraries, and administration offices represent every color of the rainbow.

Our next step is usually to tile the floors. That also gets an instantly positive response from the teachers, as suddenly it's possible to sweep their classrooms clean.

Our third step is usually to put glass in the windows, and that too makes a big difference as to how both teachers and students feel about their school.[5]

As I said, we are careful not to step on any toes. We are adopting government schools, not building private ones, so we feel it's best not to tamper with what's already in place. In Spien Chrieve, for example, we retained the existing principal and all the teachers, although we did ask the local Ministry of Education for additional teachers in anticipation of the school's population swelling once the new building was completed. We started to realize that there was a buzz in the community about the sparkling new building that was being constructed. It was the early stages of the energy and passion that would soon percolate in Spien Chrieve about our work there.

Some teachers warmed to us more quickly than others, however. One of our toughest challenges was Chok Dary, the school's principal, born to a Thai father and a Cambodian mother. Before the Khmer Rouge took power her father had been a well-known lawyer in the community and well connected to many people in government. The family had lived in a large house not far from where the Amelio School now stands.

When it became clear that Pol Pot was going to take over, her father wanted to move the entire family to Thailand, where they would be safe. He actually had the visas in hand, but Dary's mother, whose parents and brothers and sisters all lived nearby, had second thoughts. Once the

---

5. In 2008, after a school collapsed in Haiti killing more than ninety people, shoring up the roof and making certain it was safe became our first priority.

Khmer Rouge took over it was too late. The family was marched into the countryside to a life of slave labor. Like most professionals, Dary's father was killed. Dary was in her early twenties by this time, and as the oldest child she felt responsible for the family and never married.

After the Khmer Rouge was finally expelled and the United Nations occupied Cambodia to administer free elections, the family built a bamboo hut on a small piece of land not far from where Dary had grown up. Savy was actually a boarder in the house when he first arrived in Siem Reap. Dary and her mom still get tears in their eyes when they drive by the old homestead.

When I first met Dary she had two jobs. She was the school principal, but also had an administrative job with the local Ministry of Education so that she had the advantage of a more regular paycheck. Her entire family worked tremendously hard. Dary and her mother also sold Khmer rice noodles and pickled fish to be able to afford to send Dary's younger brother and sister to school.

More than a year went by before Dary warmed to me personally, and it took another year after that for us to convince her to leave her Department of Education job and work exclusively at our school in Spien Chrieve. In fact, only after we started our teacher training and Food for Thought programs (explained in subsequent chapters) did she start poking her head into our planning meetings to see what we were up to. Perhaps that's when she started to believe we might really be doing something meaningful.

Today Dary is one of our best spokespersons, representing us at conferences and various CFC training sessions. She has become an important part of the CFC family, so much so that a few years ago when she needed emergency surgery, CFC paid to send her to a hospital in Phnom Penh.

Chok Dary, our Amelio School principal.

Our First School Opens

On October 24, 2003, the Amelio School, named for Bill's mother Mary who had passed away a year earlier, was officially unveiled on what would have been her sixty-seventh birthday. The construction and renovation had taken fewer than five months.

Attending the opening day ceremonies were the governor of Siem Reap, the minister of education from the Siem Reap province, various community leaders, Chok Dary, and virtually every teacher, plus at least half the village, hundreds of children, and curious staff from a number of surrounding schools. Bill and I were also there, along with our children and a contingent of volunteers from Singapore. You could really feel the enthusiasm of the audience and their happiness and pride in this new school and this special moment.

During the ceremony, which began with a Buddhist blessing, we sat on plastic white chairs in the original thatched hut building. The day was glorious, a wonderful celebration that combined the traditions of East and West.

Six monks in orange robes held flowers as they walked through the main entrance of the campus. They offered their blessings while laying a bouquet of magnificent lotus and tuberose blossoms at our feet. We had been instructed not to touch the monks or even meet their gazes, so we were careful to sit very quietly, looking off into the distance. They walked off the makeshift stage in perfect stillness, perfect in every way.

Traditional Cambodian dancers then performed, moving beautifully among the villagers who sat all around the schoolyard. They put on a fabulous show, chanting in their native Khmer tongue. This was followed by speeches by the governor, the *chau sangkart*, and Principal Dary. Savy and I also spoke a few words.

The speeches by the adults went on a bit too long, of course, but then every child was handed a school uniform inside a backpack, all donated by families from SAS. In yet another piece of serendipity, I realized the American school uniforms of white shirts and blue shorts that represented most of my circle were identical to those worn by Cambodian children. No wonder it had been so easy to get donated uniforms from SAS!

The day's finale was unforgettable. Following a beautiful Cambodian tradition, doves were released from a birdcage into the open air and disappeared high into the sky, signifying a new beginning. Then in our wonderful Western way, we cut the ceremonial ribbon so that everyone from dignitary to child could enter the Amelio School for the first time.

Operational Challenges

On the first day of school, hundreds of children attended grades one through six, an increase of about forty percent from the previous year. The jump made us realize just how many children had not been going to school before we arrived. Today, enrollment in the Amelio School exceeds seven hundred students.

We faced a number of challenges those first months. There was nothing we could do about the government failing to pay our teachers on time or sometimes not at all, but we could make it clear that no child would have to pay to go to school. That was something we would not tolerate, although it wasn't easy to put a complete stop to it. Thankfully, this has changed over time, but not before Savy made an example of some of the teachers and had them transferred to a non-CFC school for trying to take money from the kids.

A big breakthrough came once we decided to pay our teachers a stipend to supplement their modest government salary. This way they were guaranteed something even if the government didn't pay them. Over the years, experience has taught us not to give the same amount of money to a teacher who is disinterested and uninvolved as one who is creative and hardworking. Today in all our schools we use an incentive-based graded pay system, whereby stipends are directly linked to how well a teacher performs.[6]

Our accounting system has since become much more professional, but for the first year or two I would wire Savy money and he would dole out the appropriate amount of cash to each teacher. He had a clipboard

---

6.   See Salary Bonus Criteria Observation Sheet in Appendix A.

with the names of each teacher and administrative staff, and when he handed them cash they would sign next to their name to acknowledge receipt of the funds. Unlike the government, we were on time *every* month, further solidifying our foundation of trust. It was all very efficient and organized, and my esteem for Savy, as well as my recognition of the incredible good fortune that had brought him to CFC, continued to grow.

Nonetheless, we have to be constantly vigilant against various forms of minor corruption. I wanted to trust people in the same way I was hoping they would trust me, but years of darkness had created some difficult, hard-to-break habits. Sometimes we just looked the other way, but other times we could not, as when Savy gave each teacher at the Amelio School petty cash to buy supplies for their classrooms and a few of them failed to return with the pencils, chalk, and notebooks they had been asked to purchase.

We didn't have the authority to fire anyone, certainly not in these early days, but we found ways to show our displeasure. It was a long time before any of the teachers who had pocketed the petty cash ever received funds from CFC again. Even today, we can only strongly suggest that a truly unmotivated or dishonest teacher be reassigned to a non-CFC school. Nonetheless, teachers slowly but surely got the message that things were different at the Amelio School.

The stipend we paid, which started as low as $5 per month and has grown to more than $95 for our very best mentor teachers, was success-ful in stopping the practice of children supplementing teachers' salaries. It didn't completely solve the problem of teachers being uninspired or unqualified, however. Most teachers back in 2003 had matriculated only through a six-month teaching course, after which they were given a teaching certificate. Then they were handed hundreds of pages of gov-ernment-endorsed curriculum that typically contained one sentence of instruction, along with tests in the back of the manual that were to be given to students every ninety days. Based on the scores of the students, the local Ministry of Education would then determine whether or not these were good teachers.

This was clearly an ineffective system. The question was, how were we going to improve it?

Teacher Training

Very few of our teachers had much experience or training in how the information in the detailed curriculum could be taught in a way that was interesting for both them and the children. I'm not sure we had a single teacher with a college education. They were, after all, part of a generation that had lived in a Cambodia when there was no public school education at all. They were much more likely to have been taught to shoot a gun by the time they were ten than to have been taught to read and write. One of our best teachers, Chan Vandy, learned how to read under a tree using a rock to scrape out the alphabet and spell words in the dirt.

As real as this challenge was, our bigger battle lay in motivating our teachers. As Savy and I got to know them, we were struck by the low opinion most of them had of their profession. The most obvious example was that many of them were consistently late, leaving classrooms of kids to fend for themselves. Their jobs just did not seem particularly important to most of them, an attitude that was reflected in their performance and, most visibly, in the appearance of their classrooms.

By this time our Education Committee in Singapore was meeting at least twice a week, posing questions and brainstorming about the issues we were facing in Siem Reap. Committee members started to offer numerous suggestions about teaching methods and ways to motivate both teachers and students. Following their advice, we began to ask our teachers questions like, "What does your classroom look like?" and "Is it clean?" and "Is it orderly?"

These were very elementary questions, of course, but ones we hoped would get them started on a change in mindset. We gradually began asking questions that tried to encourage them to investigate more complex issues, such as "Are the materials that the children see in your classroom stimulating?" and "Is your room conducive to learning?" and "Is your room colorful and fun?" Gradually, blank stares were replaced by glints of recognition.

That first year we put a lot of focus on the "look" of the classrooms, on distinguishing our school as a place where learning was going to be fun and exciting. Painting the classrooms was just a start, and soon colorful images of the children's work began to cover the walls, supplemented by playful presentations of numbers and letters we imported from Singapore.

Teacher training was our biggest challenge, but we did have some teachers who immediately "got it." Almost all of them had some kind of extraordinary story. The young, always smiling Chan Vandy, for example, was in her early twenties when she started working at the Amelio School, and she was immensely excited about this new world of creative instruction being revealed to her. From the very beginning of the school year, Vandy stood out among her peers, and when things at the school started changing, so did her classroom.

Vandy and I talked a lot about what teaching meant to her and why she had become a teacher. This was the same girl who had sat under a tree and tried to learn with almost no kind of instruction. She had come to CFC as a shy young teacher, barely confident enough to talk in front of a room filled with six-year-olds. Today she walks into a classroom positively glowing with excitement, communicating to everyone her feeling of being proud of her profession.

Vandy and her colleague, Chea Sophea, are now two of our leading mentor teachers who hold weekly training meetings at each of our schools. They spend the rest of their time observing classrooms and making specific suggestions to our other teachers. They also help determine the monthly bonuses teachers receive for outstanding work.

Early on, it seemed to me that teachers who appeared disinterested and uninspired were being spiteful, but Chan Vandy made me realize this was not the case. No one had ever taught them how to teach, that it was inappropriate to take money from students, that public education was supposed to be free, or that learning could be made interesting for both teachers and students. That was *our* job, I realized, and we all now recognized that it would continue to be our biggest challenge as CFC started to think about building and adopting other schools.

One issue of particular concern to me personally was corporal punishment. I wanted to simply say to the teachers, "You *cannot* hit the children," but that was something I could not do. I was not in a position to impose Western values on these Cambodian strangers, so I had to be creative in our approach and teach them other options of disciplining students. Soon CFC would establish a formal teacher training program, but in 2003 we were trying to keep things simple, starting with other ways to get children's attention besides going up and whacking them on the side of the head.

Our Education Committee had some suggestions. If, for example, children were talking out of turn and the teacher couldn't get their attention, instead of becoming harsh and angry, she might have a prearranged sign that would shift the cycle of disruption. The teacher might clap her hands twice quickly, for example, or raise her hands over her head.

Whispering was another technique. Whispering made the kids strain to hear what the teacher was saying. Suddenly one student would stop talking, another would stop, and then another.

We learned many, many lessons early on. Birds were getting into our new building and nesting in the rafters, leaving their droppings on the floor and desks, or even dive bombing onto students' heads in the middle of a lesson. The solution, putting blocks on the windows to keep the birds out, was actually quite simple, yet even today one way to distinguish a CFC school from any other is by whether or not you see bird droppings inside the classrooms.

Of course, just the fact that the school in Spien Chrieve was housed in a sparkling new building went a long way toward making both teachers and students feel differently about their school. A school where the kids had to duck under a table when it rained had been replaced by a center for learning. That alone made a powerful statement about the value of education.

Getting Parents Involved

We also broke new ground by reaching out to the parents of our students to create an informal parent and teachers association. At first this involved just chatting up the parents when they dropped off their kids at school. Eventually it evolved into parent/teacher meetings so that they could grasp what their children were learning and see and understand the progress they were making.

We also started a tradition of having an open house for parents at the beginning of each school year. Parents now have come to expect and look forward to these events at each of our schools.

Being encouraged to participate in their children's education was a new experience for most of these families, and sometimes we had to bribe them to get them involved. We'd bring donated clothes, rice, and other food staples to school, and no one who showed up for their parent/teacher meeting or stopped by to say hello went home empty-handed. That definitely captured their attention.

Our most important realization during these early months, one that we did not even articulate to ourselves that first year, was that success—real success—would come from sustainable actions. It was one thing to build a new school or even feed a family, but change that wasn't embraced and co-opted by the community would ultimately be useless.

Many times we heard stories from Savy and others about a NGO that had arrived in Siem Reap and had given the community what Savy calls "a gift of burden," a well-meaning gift that turns into a burden. An example would be if an individual or NGO donated a school or other physical structure and then ultimately walked away, leaving the new facility with no means of making necessary repairs or upkeep.

We were committed to earning a reputation for something quite different. Any time we built a school or promised to feed children or train teachers we wanted to be sure that any gains we made would continue into the indefinite future. The way to do that was to localize our successes, with the long-term goal of turning CFC's initiatives over to the people who lived there.

We always started small. One of our most important accomplishments that first year was to convince most of our teachers of the benefits of a clean classroom. Before CFC got involved, Thursday was cleanup day, which in practice meant the classrooms were pretty much a mess every day except Friday. We planted the seed that perhaps, with the help of every student, the classrooms could be cleaned and straightened *every* day. This made a huge difference in how both students and teachers felt about their personal space.

Another successful initiative was giving away bicycles, lots and lots of bicycles. We quickly realized that almost all the children came to school by foot, sometimes from as far away as ten miles. A few children had bicycles, and they would often transport two or three other kids who hung from their shoulders or sat on the handlebars.

From the first day one of our main questions was, "How can we help get kids get to school in the first place and then keep them coming?" If we could provide a means of transportation, a big part of our challenge would be solved.

Bicycles, we soon realized, were the answer. They were a way to give a hand up, rather than a hand out.

Shortly after the Amelio School opened its doors, Savy, with the help of the teachers, administrators, and village leaders, identified the children who lived furthest from school and were most in need of a bicycle. That first year we must have distributed two hundred bikes to Amelio School students. We typically purchased twenty or thirty at a time from a vendor in the Siem Reap market, paying about $25 per bike. Then we'd load them onto a rented pickup truck and park ourselves somewhere in the middle of the village. Somehow, within minutes everyone in the area knew we were handing out bicycles, and although Savy seemed to know which families needed one most, someone in need was inevitably left without a bicycle. As is the Cambodian way, no one ever complained, and Savy always made sure they received a bicycle the next time.

Without question, the bicycles changed peoples' lives, and not just students' lives, but the lives of entire families. The bikes are used for so much more than just a ride to school. Parents can now bicycle to the market or to work, which gives them a freedom that has changed their daily lives far more than if we simply handed them food, clothing, or money. Giving a hand up rather than a hand out has become one of CFC's many mantras.

MAD Trips

Meanwhile, back in Singapore we continued to rally our troops. CFC had grown into an active, enthusiastic group of supporters, primarily American women expats. And that's still true today. Although we have some wonderful men on our board of directors, and Bill has always been a powerful, inspiring presence, CFC's nucleus of volunteers remains women. Maybe that's why I've always considered CFC an organization of emotion and passion.

At the same time, I've come to realize how important it is that our husbands support our work. I have seen long-time volunteers forced to step back when their husbands were not quite "there." Bill has always been "beyond there," as have so many of our orange friends. When the orange bleeds through to family members, it is wonderful to see.

While the Amelio School was being built, I expanded our base in Singapore by asking women I knew to lunch and showing them photographs of the Cambodian children and encouraging them to visit Siem Reap on their own to see for themselves what we were doing. CFC was also constantly organizing visits. We called them Make A Difference, or MAD, trips, and they soon evolved into something much more ambitious than bringing donations of school supplies and clothing to the schools. We began to regularly organize groups of families to go to Siem Reap to build houses in the villages that surrounded our schools, or to help with construction projects on one of our campuses. Bill also organized a number of team-building trips when he worked for Dell and later for Lenovo, an idea that spread to other multinational companies.

At first I didn't really want to be in the business of building houses because I thought it would distract from our primary mission of building and operating schools, but our volunteers were constantly asking for projects they could call their own. In response, Savy began to identify families in need and we began organizing house-building teams of volunteers directed by a Cambodian contractor, usually Mr. San.

In recent years, Mr. San has been assisted by a young man named Chea Song, whom everyone calls Tong. Under Mr. San's tutelage, Tong learned how to construct Siem Reap's typical home, built on stilts to protect the inside from the mud that appears everywhere during the rainy season. Tong has made it his personal mission to guide volunteers who have never before picked up a hammer, much less built a home or school, and instruct them how, through teamwork, they can together build a house in just a few days.

One of twelve children, Tong is a sweet, gentle young man who always seems to me to be way too skinny. I think he gives all his hard-earned CFC money to his family instead of using some of it to feed himself. He has become a local role model, looked up to by his family and villagers, another example of an angel dropped at the CFC doorstep.

Austin and our nephew Nick Amelio with Mr. San (far right), his crew and our wonderful Tong (next to Austin). This was Austin's life-changing trip.

Our house-building prowess has definitely improved over the years, mostly through trial and error. The first home we built was in 2003 near the Amelio School. We used an assembly line to pass buckets of water from person to person until someone at the end of the line mixed the cement. It was like an old-fashioned fire brigade, but it wasn't very efficient, and our volunteers were heartbroken when they had to leave before the house was finished.

We learned from our mistakes. Now the family that will occupy the new home readies the site with the help of their neighbors before our volunteers arrive. They clear the land and cart away the remnants of any existing structure. Usually the Cambodians also dig holes for the wooden posts and steady them with fresh cement. They sometimes even frame out the walls. With this kind of preparation, our volunteers, if they put in twelve-hour days, can complete a house during a three-day visit, although the stairs and floors sometimes have to be installed later.

Anyone who has been part of these home-building trips will tell you how amazing it is to actually go deep into a village that most tourists never see and to work side by side with Cambodians to build someone a home. It is a life-changing experience that combines ancient knowledge and skills with modern know-how, all made possible by dedicated man and womanpower.

The process also gives CFC volunteers a unique peek into Cambodian family life, which is a fascinating blend of East and West. The walls of most Cambodian homes are made from an intricate weaving of palm leaves and wires sewn together very tightly. At one point we tried to suggest using other methods, but we never could make a good case for anything that was sturdier than their age-old tradition.

These MAD trips became another important way to not only get our volunteers connected to what we were doing in Siem Reap, but also to demonstrate that we were not about building a school or a home and then walking away. Our volunteers, in turn, came to understand that you don't have to be a contractor to go in and rebuild a life. Instead, you can be an ordinary—no, extraordinary—human being who, under normal circumstances never picks up a hammer, but just this once makes a difference in a different way.

71

That's part of what makes building a home for someone such an incredible experience. As an organization, it solidifies our standing in the community, making our efforts truly meaningful in people's lives. CFC promises to stay and to come back and we do. We build the buildings. We train the teachers. We construct the houses. We help the families. We educate the kids. And we keep coming back to make sure we're helping. That's our promise to ourselves and to our partners in Cambodia—the children and their teachers and their families.

A Year of Discovery

Looking back on that first year, we were proud of our accomplishments, but we also recognized many things that needed fixing. For me personally, I needed to start listening to Savy more and talking less. My mind was like a speeding car. I had so many ideas I was throwing out left and right. "Let's do this . . . let's do that." For me, it was all very emotionally driven, but I finally got it. I saw that it was essential that I slow down and listen to Savy's advice and let things start working, really working, at their own pace.

"You know things are happening," he assured me at the close of the Amelio School's first year. "Children are learning. Let's keep going."

I soon started giving similar advice to Savy until "Talk less do more" became our own private coded message. Over the years Savy and I have heard hundreds of people talk, talk, talk. We have decided we prefer doing to talking.

While we did not have an official closing day ceremony that first year, Savy and I and some of the teachers and volunteers brought in food for an informal celebration. Parents came in and out and there was a real sense of community. Everyone knew we had taken a huge step forward.

We could see it on the children's faces and in the requests by their parents to "Please do more. Please be more." And that's what we committed to do.

2003 was a tumultuous year for me on another front too. At the same time Bill and I and so many others were working hard to solidify CFC as an organization prepared for the long term, I was also monitoring my ailing mother in San Antonio. She was suffering from Alzheimer's, and as anyone who has had a family member with this horrible disease knows, it can be just as hard on the family as the patient. I spoke to her every few days and spent as much time with her as I could during my trips back to Texas. Bill traveled there regularly on business and always made an effort to see her. My mother loved Bill, and was always saying how much my father would have appreciated his tough-love personality.

Strangely enough, there were moments when I was thankful my mother didn't realize I was so far away. We all knew the end was near, and during Christmas break I went home to see her and to celebrate a wonderful year, but instead found myself planning her funeral. Somehow I felt like she had waited for me to come home to die.

My sister Veronica was with her when she passed; I arrived an hour later and was able to give her one last kiss goodbye. As usual, Bill was by my side, my rock who helped me get through a rough week with my head up. Amanda sang at the funeral and graveside in a beautiful service that my mom would have been proud of. In fact, I believe she was.

FIVE

Teaching the Teachers

After the success of the Amelio School we knew we wanted to replicate CFC's reach into other schools in the Siem Reap area. We were not done, not by a long shot.

As always, Savy had his ear to the ground and during the summer of 2004 he learned that one of the elementary schools that served Bakong, an extremely poor village about fourteen kilometers north of Siem Reap, was being forced to shut down by the Cambodian government.

The children there had been attending a school next to a Buddhist temple, but suddenly the government had decided to enforce a law prohibiting any school from operating on the grounds of a temple. With a new school year approaching, many children had nowhere to go.

Savy used the same negotiating strategies that had worked in Spien Chrieve.

"We'll build you a school, support it with supplies and volunteer labor, and provide the teachers with a cash stipend," he told Bakong's community leaders. "All we need is the land on which to build."

We even had a site picked out, a large vacant piece of land next to an existing school. Only later did we realize we'd have to construct a fence around the campus to keep out the oxen grazing nearby.

To show our good intentions, we invited Bakong's leaders to visit the Amelio School, which was already beginning to look and sound very different from the typical Cambodian school. They must have been impressed because the site we chose was almost immediately approved for our use.

Once again Mr. San and his crew, using the same architectural plans from the World Bank, built a simple one-story, five-room structure.

Originally we also intended to renovate the existing building, but upon investigation we realized the foundation and cement floors were terribly cracked and that termites were having a daily feast on the roof. The building seemed to be just one bite from total collapse, so we ended up almost completely rebuilding it from scratch.

Thirty thousand dollars goes a long way in Cambodia, and we were able to complete both buildings in just under five months. Once again we were a bit amazed to be within budget and on time in a country the world considered highly corrupt.

In November of 2004 the Bakong School was ready for students. Patterned after the previous year's festivities at Amelio, we celebrated another opening day highlighted by Buddhist prayers and a ribbon-cutting ceremony.

We also replicated our successful program of distributing bicycles, and this proved even more critical in Bakong, a village spread across more than a dozen kilometers. Very few people in Bakong own cars so most people buy or barter their daily necessities from makeshift market stalls outside individual homes. Many villagers go years without venturing more than a few kilometers from home. The gift of a two-wheeled non-motorized vehicle not only allowed children to get to school, but also gave their parents easy access to Siem Reap proper.

The Home Front

On the home front I found life increasingly hectic. I continued to fly back and forth a couple of times each month between Singapore and Siem Reap, and Bill was traveling even more frequently once he was named CEO of Lenovo at the end of 2005. Women talk about the balancing act between work and being a mother, but I never considered myself to be juggling work and family because CFC had become part of my family. Particularly for Riley and Bronson, CFC had become a regular part of their lives, like homework or summers in Austin. Their mom's full-time job, usually done from home, just happened to sometimes include them being whisked off to Siem Reap for a weekend or during spring break to help distribute supplies, clear a field, or build a school.

In 2004, partly in response to challenges we were having with our oldest son, Bill and I added a new member to our household, our nephew Anthony from Pittsburgh. Anthony was Bill's brother's son and Austin's pal, and his parents thought it would be a great experience for him to spend a year in Asia. We hoped he would be a good influence on Austin, who was now seventeen and seriously rebellious. Bill was traveling Mondays through Fridays most weeks, and I took both teenagers to Siem Reap with me several times that year hoping it would do them some good.

Looking back, both boys say that seeing how Cambodians lived and helping to build desperately-needed houses and schools planted a seed that eventually taught them to appreciate the privilege of their birth. They may have rolled their eyes each time Bill or I reminded them that, "To whom much is given, much is expected," but once they entered young adulthood they admitted their experiences in Siem Reap profoundly impacted them. In fact, Austin often says that Cambodia saved his life, but that's a story for a little later.

Avery

To make my life even more complicated, by the time Bakong School was ready to open in late 2004 I was eight months pregnant and receiving a lot of flack from friends and family for continuing my frequent trips to Siem Reap. Yet somehow, in spite of all the craziness, CFC and the Amelio family pushed forward with a lot of optimism. My relationship with Cambodia had taken on a life of its own and so had CFC's growth spurt. With the help of some key women in Singapore, and Savy of course, CFC was making a difference in the lives of more and more people.

Typical of the many volunteers whose commitment ran deep was Lori McConaghy, who later received a Golden Hand award and took on several roles at once, including secretary of the CFC board and frequent visitor to Siem Reap. I started to cry one day when her daughter Alex, who was about ten at the time, came over to the house and handed me the money she had raised at a toy sale she had conducted at their condo complex.

Just as I was certain Austin and Anthony would ultimately benefit from our frequent trips to Siem Reap, I was equally confident things would be all right with my pregnancy. As it turned out, on January 5, 2005, Bill and I became the parents of a beautiful baby girl delivered at the Mt. Elizabeth Hospital in Singapore.

Once I resumed my weekend trips to Cambodia, Baby Avery became my constant companion. She must have visited the schools in either Bakong or Spien Chrieve a dozen times before her first birthday. As any new parent knows, it's a lot easier to travel with an infant than with a three- or four-year-old, and as a breastfeeding mom, Avery and I were literally inseparable. In Cambodia that meant she seemed to be part of me, since any time we were outdoors in the overwhelming heat she was stuck to me with sweat.

Avery was a huge hit among the Cambodians. To them, she seemed huge and extremely white and endlessly fascinating. She was a great conversation starter. Cambodians are not a touchy people, but any time I got to talking to a mom or a teacher or a student, they invariably wanted to hold Avery, or at least stroke her hair. Avery was extremely shy, so she just held on to me more tightly.

Austin

Not everything was so cheerful back in Singapore. Halfway through Austin's junior year in high school I started to admit to myself that he had a drinking problem.

"I was partying as hard as I possibly could," he now admits. "At that point there was no way my parents were going to be able to control me."

No kidding.

On some level I must have been in denial because it took me a while to realize how bad Austin's drinking had become. By the end of his junior year he was partying and passing out almost every other night. The final straw occurred one Sunday morning when he woke up on top of the ten-foot-high fence that separated our property from our neighbor's. Apparently he had been trying to climb over the gate to get home and had blacked out. The wall wasn't very wide on top so he must have spent the night curled up in a ball, lucky not to roll off.

Anthony remembers Austin stumbling into the kitchen the next morning and seeing Bill, who immediately announced, "Good! You're up in time for church."

Anthony and Austin thought that was hysterical, and it *has* since become part of our family lore, but it wasn't funny at the time.

I knew I needed to get Austin help. With CFC, I had always said that failure wasn't an option, that we would do everything we could to make sure the organization was always moving forward toward a better place. Bill and I had made a commitment to each other and to hundreds of people in Cambodia that what we were doing was going to have legs, that it would never become a gift of burden. That meant making a long-term commitment not to accept anything less than sustainable success. Now I took that same attitude to get help for my son.

Austin and I had gone through a lot together; we had a history longer and filled with more drama than anyone else in the family. Long before I had met Bill, back in Texas, it had just been the two of us. Some of the memories were hard, like trying to get Austin back into happy mode when Kenny was a no-show, or even just taking him to a restaurant. Austin was always all over the place, while other kids sat calmly in their high chairs. I remember thinking, *Really? What's wrong with those other four-year-olds? Did their parents drug them or something?*

Still, most of our early times together were great. Before Austin's first birthday I was taking him with me to my job at the health club. At the nursery there he started speaking Spanish before English. Driving to work we used to sing together at the top of our lungs to U2, Tom Petty, Erasure, Yaz, and Madonna.

Bill embraced Austin just about the day they met, and the first time Austin called Bill "Dad" I hid my tears from both of them. And I'll never forget handing Austin his brother the day Riley was born. Austin was eight, and I thought Bill and my mother were going to pass out.

These memories were all rocketing through me as I asked the advice of a number of experts and began to understand that Austin was in serious need of help. We had to do something immediately, both because the problem had become so severe and because we wanted to act while he was still a minor. We needed to do something dramatic that would jolt him out of what had become his routine of drinking. We decided on a surprise intervention before sending him to a rehab center in the United States.

There were a million other things going on at the time as well. It was the end of the school year and I was getting Bronson and Riley ready for their field day at school. Dee Gallo, a good friend who had become one of CFC's most active supporters and our human resources guru, was moving, which added to the stress.

Still, nothing was more important than getting Austin help. I was in turmoil, taking care of all the details, and then suddenly it was happening. I handled all the arrangements up until that June moment he stepped onto the plane. Bill, thank God, would handle the most difficult part.

The two of them flew to Pittsburgh together. Austin thought he was going to spend time with Anthony, who by now had graduated from high school and had moved back to the U.S., and that Bill was going to spend time with his father and brother.

They stayed the first night at Pap's house, which is what Austin calls Bill's dad. At 4:00 a.m. the doorbell rang. A groggy, jet-lagged Austin was in the kitchen eating a banana when Bill opened the door and ushered in two burly gentlemen, who Austin immediately mistook for law enforcement. One actually was an off-duty policeman.

"I didn't know what was going on," Austin remembers. "I was so out of it I think I offered them a banana. I turned to my dad and asked him what was happening, and I saw tears in his eyes and suddenly I was in handcuffs. I was scared and confused. I just remember yelling, 'Dad, what the f is going on?' A second ago I was eating a banana!"

Bill told Austin we had decided that an intensive rehab center was the only solution to help him with what had become a serious addiction, and that he wouldn't be returning to Singapore without getting some help.

The next thing Austin knew two men were leading him through the Pittsburgh airport. "I'm sure people thought I was a fugitive," he says now. "I sat in the middle seat between the two men the whole way to Dahlonega, Georgia."

As for me, back in Singapore with our other children, that was a night I will never forget. That night I came to understand the power of "physical emotion." I was ill with sadness and fear for my son, but I knew that if we didn't do something Austin could kill himself drinking.

Austin spent his first two days in solitary confinement before settling into the center's routine of awakening at 6:00 a.m., running six miles, eating breakfast, working out, and then spending the rest of the day in a group session with other addicts he referred to as "crazy people."

"I was in shock the first week or two," he remembers. "Some people were hooked on PCP; others were heroin addicts. I had never been exposed to anything like that. I was scared, but I was raised by my dad to be tough and that carried me through. We were in the middle of meth country and were warned not to venture out. The place was like Alcatraz in that we were told if we tried to escape, we'd perish. Instead of drowning, we'd be picked up by sketchy meth lab criminals. I still don't know if any of that was true, but I believed it at the time."

Austin hadn't yet hit bottom, but I do think his seven weeks in Dahlonega helped give him some perspective. He had to write in a journal every day and that, combined with the group sessions, at least made him confront reality, and a few of his emotions. But he still didn't think he had a problem. As it turned out, that was his biggest problem.

He was happy to see us when it was all over, however. He had been hiking thirteen to fifteen miles a day with a full pack and all he had eaten were army meals out of a can. The first thing he asked was if we could go to the Jack in the Box restaurant down the road. He seemed fit but super fragile. I felt equally fragile. Was my son better? Only time would tell.

A Second Wind

We all returned to Singapore in August of 2005 hopeful that Austin had turned a corner, but unfortunately he soon fell back into bad habits. I was in over my head, coping with Austin, managing CFC, traveling back and forth from Singapore to Siem Reap with a new baby, and being a mom to Bronson and Riley. In fact, the week Austin checked into rehab I sent a note to my CFC team telling them I had to step back for just a bit. I had never done that before and haven't done it since, but fortunately things were slow that summer. More importantly, and not surprisingly, my orange team came through for me.

That's the wonder of our orange volunteers. So many people have taken on the same intense passion. The volunteers I have met over the years have proven over and over what angels do. I know it's a cliché, but yes, volunteers *are* angels with invisible wings. I have seen people give so much that I cry when I think of it. On one trip one of our most active volunteers, Bob Brundage, was bitten by a rabid dog, but even that didn't slow him down.

Sometimes when I felt most worn down, or feared I had taken on an impossible task, something would happen that inspired me all over again. In fact, I constantly found ways to get re-centered and reenergized.

Sometimes I cleared my head by taking a day by myself at the temples. Walking in silence through the ruins of Angkor Wat and Angkor Thom, or the less frequented temples like Chapel of the Hospital or Banteay Srey, allowed me to imagine the bustle of these places a thousand years ago, something you cannot do anywhere else in the world. You can't walk up next to the pyramids in Egypt and touch them. In Siem Reap, you're *in* them. You can feel the mystical energy of what went on there.

Any time I questioned the task I had taken on I tried not to get ahead of myself. I played little games in my head, telling myself, *Just relax; people do this all over the world. They go and do something different.* I would push logic against emotion, telling myself repeatedly, *I'm not going to let this go. The status quo here is not okay.*

I also spent a lot of time at the schools and accompanying Savy when he visited people's homes to reinforce the lessons the children were learning. One family I'll never forget was ostracized by others in the community. They were considered cursed because several members of the family had a lazy eye, which is actually a lay term for amblyopia, a childhood condition that occurs when one eye is weaker than the other.

I remember walking up a rickety ladder into their home, removing my shoes, and sitting with them on the mud floor. The mother welcomed me, as she walked nervously around the house, a bamboo shack on stilts, gathering her kids' belongings and asking me if I wanted a drink or a snack, just like I would if a stranger visited *my* home. We sat drinking through the same straw placed inside a single coconut, and the shared humanity of that moment filled me with hope and perspective.

Whenever I struggled with a sense of hopelessness something like this would happen to career me back into optimism. This family was hopeful in spite of their situation and that made me feel that together we could really do something.

For many months remembering this moment kept me going, and I have never again offered someone a glass of wine without thinking of sitting with that family. The memory never goes away and I can conjure it up—the desperation, the heartache, and the equally big feelings of raw emotion. We have so much and they have so little, but it's the same all over the world in any size home. The woman with the lazy-eyed children loves them just as much as I love my kids, and in the same exact way wants what's best for them.

One of the girls in that family, Manoot, also has a case of palsy; one side of her face is paralyzed. She became an Amelio School dancer, and when the dance troupe visited Singapore in 2005, she was one of the children who stayed at our house. I thought she would be the most nervous and reserved child who visited, but wow, she was the funniest and most outgoing of the group. Wearing makeup and her beautiful dance outfit transformed Manoot. She was no longer the girl with the paralyzed face and the cursed family. She was the most gorgeous girl ever. Before, I had seen only a little girl with half her face paralyzed, trying to hide her smile, but the bubbly had always been there.

Other huge lessons came when I walked or drove through the villages in a deliberate effort to remind myself why I was there and why I had to keep going. The oxen under the houses. The burning garbage. Dogs everywhere, hanging out with chickens. These are the kinds of memories that caught me, kept me, haunted me. If ever I felt like giving up, these feelings stopped me because they never ever left. I might be exhausted and unable to think, worried that my family needed me, that my friends were wondering when I would slow down, but then I would think of the individual children and their families who now relied on CFC.

Over the years it has been hard to accept that CFC can't save everyone, but it's good to know we have saved some. During one early visit to Spien Chrieve I watched a young child, David, crawl toward us down the dusty road. In Cambodia the disabled are rarely encouraged to get an education, but I insisted David attend one of our CFC schools. We brought over a pair of orthopedic shoes from Singapore to correct his club feet, and today David plays at recess just like any other child.

Austin and David, 2005.

Every time I got on a plane to return to Singapore, these are the stories I remembered. During this time when I was having so much trouble with Austin's partying and drinking, this was also the kind of thing I wanted him to witness, so I took him with me to Cambodia as often as I could to show him people like Manoot and David.

"Don't you get it?" I wanted to ask him, but he didn't get it until it was his time to get it, so I just pushed forward on all fronts—at home, in Singapore, and in Siem Reap.

Not all my experiences in Cambodia were so uplifting, of course. One fall day in October of 2004 I experienced the ferociousness of Cambodia's rainy season for the first time. I was with Savy in a tiny car he had borrowed, on our way to buy equipment for the new computer lab we were opening in Spien Chrieve. We were driving over one of the small bridges that cross the Siem Reap River when suddenly we found ourselves in the midst of a flash flood. In moments the water had reached my window and the car had begun to turn on its side. We jumped out and managed to find dry land, but for a moment it flashed through my mind that we'd better open our next school before I was in the grave. Knowing how much there was to do, I vowed to work even harder.

On that same trip Savy and I returned to our schools to assess the water damage. We were standing by the same bridge when we saw the body of a small boy floating down the river.

"Is that what I think it is?" I asked Savy, who said very matter-of-factly, "Oh, yeah. He probably fell in upstream."

We could both plainly see the little boy floating on his back. His face was huge on a tiny body, his eyes bulging. That memory really freaked me out and it was years before I could drive across that particular bridge again.

Training the Teachers

In CFC's first two years we made enormous progress on a variety of fronts. We built two beautiful schools and a teacher training center in Spien Chrieve, the first of its kind in Siem Reap. We were making sure the students in both Spien Chrieve and Bakong had supplies, new uniforms, backpacks, and teachers who mostly showed up on time and did not demand payment from the children. Many of the students now rode a bicycle to school.

We also had partial control of another school in the village of Kravaan, the first school I had visited, and were looking at other communities in an effort to decide where to expand next.

We had spent a lot of time and effort building relationships—between Savy and me, and between the two of us and the teachers, the administrative staff, the children, their parents, governmental officials, and our swelling number of volunteers and supporters in Singapore and the United States.

As a result, CFC was having a growing influence on the way the schools were being run. Yet something was missing. The feeling was gnawing at me that we were making advancements on the exterior of things, while everything on the interior was staying the same.

Let me explain what I mean.

While the infrastructure at the Amelio School and soon Bakong had improved tremendously, the reality on the ground had largely stayed the same. Yes, the classrooms were cleaner and most teachers now showed up on time, but the learning had not changed. The teachers were still teaching the same way and the children continued to be dirty, hungry, and largely disinterested.

The problem wasn't the curriculum, introduced by UNICEF in the 1980s and now sanctioned by Cambodia's Ministry of Education. It's a standard curriculum of reading, writing, and arithmetic used successfully worldwide. Of course, how effectively the curriculum is taught varies widely depending on the skills and excitement of the teaching, and it was those behaviors we were concerned with.

Savy and I spent hours talking about how to make the changes we had already installed go deeper. We were fortunate to have the advice of our swelling group of expatriates in Singapore. Led by the remarkable Annie Meyer Stowell, beginning right after the New Year holidays in 2004 and continuing into late winter and early spring, our Education Committee met regularly to discuss how to improve the teaching, and by extension the learning, at our CFC schools.

The committee quickly identified the problems that had been staring us in the face for the better part of two years. Our Cambodian teachers at our schools in Spien Chrieve and Bakong knew they were supposed to convey to the children the information in the textbook, but they had no idea how to do it, much less how to employ any innovative teaching techniques. In order for CFC to take the next step in improving our schools, we needed to instill a philosophy of classroom management and learning and give the teachers new skills so they could put these ideas into practice. In other words, we needed to take it upon ourselves to teach the teachers.

This was a tall order, and we were fortunate to have a group of women with considerable experience in early childhood education. The volunteer with the most relevant experience was probably Liz King. She was a friend of Annie's, and like many of us, her children attended the Singapore American School. Liz had taught in public and private schools in the U.S. and had a master's degree in education psychology from the University of California at Berkeley. Other early members of the Education Committee included Erin Hopper, a fantastic teacher at the Singapore American School, and Eleni Scheidt, a real go-getter, who was always asking what needed to be done and then making certain it happened.

Another volunteer with extensive teaching experience was Katie Samson from the Tanglin Trust School, the British school in Singapore, who started volunteering with CFC in a small way, but eventually, and thankfully, dove deep when she realized the huge impact her personal touch and teaching experience could make. She continues to add depth and knowledge to CFC's educational programs today.

This remarkable group of women—the CFC Education Committee— were mostly the spouses of men who had been transferred to Singapore. Liz's husband, for example, worked for the U.S. government and was attached to the embassy in Singapore. Natalie Bastow, who the following year would begin to have a huge impact on CFC's growth, was in Singapore because her husband had been transferred there by UPS. Many of us had children in one of the English language schools in Singapore (a community in itself) and were looking for something constructive to do with our spare time. Others simply found out about CFC by word of mouth, and once they visited the CFC schools became inspired to get involved. These amazing women caught the bug as strongly as I had.

As part of its research, the Education Committee made two trips to Siem Ream in the spring of 2005 to observe the teachers in their classrooms at both the Amelio and Bakong Schools. They also spent a lot of time with Savy discussing the most pressing challenges at the schools and the areas that might most readily be improved.

The problems were pretty overwhelming, but in the big picture we could see what needed to be done. The problems were so vast that we adopted the phrase "bird by bird," from the title of one of Liz's favorite books by Anne Lamott. The phrase simply means to start small and take it one step at a time. As Lamott's father once advised her ten-year-old brother who was agonizing over a book report on birds, "Just take it bird by bird."

After its site visit, back in Singapore the Education Committee began to ready some new recommendations, beginning with a few brick and mortar issues like improving the poor lighting in the classrooms and replacing the existing chalkboards, which were just about unusable.

It helped, I think, that Liz had experience in the inner city schools in Washington DC, where she had worked for the Center for Artistry in Teaching (today the Center for Inspired Teaching), whose mission is to expand and enhance professional development and teacher training in the DC public schools. We all came to recognize the many similarities between the challenges faced in schools in rural Cambodia and those found in inner city America, despite the fact that they are literally worlds apart.

Most importantly, we realized that beyond any physical improvements, teaching methods had to be improved in order to better engage the children. We fully recognized that to transfer the experience of our Education Committee members to Siem Reap was going to be a tremendous challenge, but we also knew this was the only way to raise the standards of our

CFC schools. Consequently, we began to set a course that would allow us to begin training the teachers on the ground in Cambodia.

The Education Committee spent several months developing a straightforward, practical teacher training manual based on the curriculum issued by Cambodia's Ministry of Education that was used in every school in Cambodia. Kaye Bach and Katie Samson in particular spent hours together planning the most important lessons we wanted to convey and strategizing how best to communicate them. This is also when our teacher training program grew some serious roots, with the added help of teachers from the Tanglin Trust School, led by Katie Samson, Aby Beynon, Helen Kaye, Diane Ayers, and Jennifer Madge.

The idea was to show teachers a better way to teach their students. We had ambitious goals. We wanted to create an educational program that abided by the Cambodian government's requirements, while at the same time became a model of teaching that could be replicated everywhere in the country.

The members of the Education Committee began by creating lesson plans and materials and preparing general advice about how to teach the required subjects creatively. They ended up creating lesson plans for most of the school's subjects, spelling out each day's content and the strategy for teaching it. Our aim was to move our Cambodian teachers away from their "chalk and talk" teaching tradition of standing up at the chalkboard and lecturing while the students stared back at them. We were fortunate to have volunteers experienced in early childhood education to help direct these efforts.

"In my graduate school program, everything was based on observation, analysis, and problem solving," Liz remembers. "That was the same strategy we took in making our recommendations and then implementing them into our teacher training."

Once the Education Committee had developed its materials, we were ready to conduct our first teacher training session in Siem Reap. In these first informal training sessions we took the first baby steps in what would ultimately become a full-fledged formal program. We were all determined to make this work because we knew that better teaching was crucial to CFC's success.

I never went a day without searching, digging, brainstorming better ways to help out. In the end it was always the same for CFC—education, building relationships, keeping commitments, coming back. But now it was also about training the teachers. We could give the kids clean clothes, feed them, and teach them how to brush their teeth, but the truth became apparent early on that if the teachers were not on board and dedicated to actually teaching their students, none of the rest would matter.

We started by simply sharing with our Cambodian teachers the lesson plans we had developed and then showing them games and team-building exercises that in small but constructive ways could help them improve how they presented specific topics within the curriculum. Our goal was to demonstrate the effectiveness of interactions between teachers and students and among the students themselves.

To teach young children numbers, for example, we suggested that the teachers take them outside the classrooms and pair them off in teams to count rocks, shells, sticks, and anything else they could find in their natural environment. It was exciting to hear the children's laughter and chatter as they made the connection between numbers and counting by playing simple games to make sure they and their teammates had an equal number of small smooth stones. Over time, the teachers became as engaged as the students. It was liberating for them to realize they could have fun while doing genuine good for their children and their country.

Kaye to the Rescue

Still, progress was sluggish. The simple idea of preparing a lesson plan was a totally new concept for almost all our Cambodian teachers, and many of them were slow to catch on. It was a lot to take in during a single teacher training session held just once every few months, and after our first few sessions we had only scratched the surface and had admittedly barely made any inroads with most of the teachers. We quickly realized it was going to take a lot more to overcome at least two generations of outdated, ineffective teaching methods.

Then Kaye Bach came to our rescue. A New Zealander, Kaye had considerable teaching experience both as a teacher herself and as a teacher training specialist providing professional development for trainees at teacher training colleges throughout New Zealand. She had gained certification in TESSOL (Teaching English to Students of Other Languages) and had established an English language unit within an elementary school in Auckland, where she had been responsible for teaching new immigrant children, predominantly from Korea, Vietnam, and China.

Luckily for us, in 2000 Kaye's husband George had been hired by SAS and they and their two children had moved to Singapore. The following year Kaye started teaching first grade at SAS and quickly became one of the school's most beloved teachers.

Liz King, whose son was in Kaye's class, was one of Kaye's biggest fans. "Within five minutes of meeting Kaye, you knew she was orange," says Liz.

Below, Kaye explains her own orange moment:

> One weekend during spring break in 2006 George and I
> decided to visit Cambodia on holiday with some friends.
> Our daughter was in college but our son Cameron was

with us. A colleague from SAS suggested I get in touch with Savy. We corresponded by email and Savy invited me to visit the CFC schools.

I asked Savy what we could bring with us and he suggested either rice or stationary supplies. Once in Siem Reap we loaded two large duffel bags of supplies into a tuk-tuk. Upon our arrival at the Amelio School we were immediately surrounded by twenty, maybe thirty small children no more than five or six years old.

As my family and I handed the supplies over to the school's principal, unable to communicate with the children in any language, to the mortification of George and Cam I spontaneously broke into the most Western song I could think of, "If You're Happy and You Know It Clap Your Hands." I don't know what came over me but the kids were delighted by my antics and immediately joined in, even though they spoke no English.

I was hooked. From just about the moment my feet touched the Cambodian soil I knew I was going back. Without a doubt, I was going back. As for so many of us, it was almost a spiritual experience without having anything to do with religion. It was my "orange moment."

On the same, trip Kaye was surprised to learn from Savy that her friend Liz King was deeply involved with CFC. Standing in the Amelio School's schoolyard, she called Liz on her cell phone. "I need to talk to you about this," she told her. "Something is happening here and I want to know about it and be part of it."

By this time, Annie Meyer Stowell's husband had been transferred back to the States so Liz had become our new Education Committee chair.

Other key players at this juncture were Katie Samson, Erin Hopper, Jenny Redlin, and Sarah Farris.

One of Kaye's earliest contributions was to articulate what the rest of us were already thinking: that we needed to step up the pace if we wanted our lessons to stick. She called it the "Three Times Rule" and she believed it applied to most learning situations, not just those in Cambodia.

"Any training you do needs to be done three times," Kaye explains. "The first time teachers hear it but have no understanding. The second time they hear it there's a little comprehension but don't expect the lessons to be carried out in the classroom. The third time they hear it they understand it and you will begin to see evidence of it in their teaching."

Kaye and a few other women, including Katie Samson, made several more trips to Siem Reap to see for themselves what was needed. Kaye has a very clear memory of what she saw because it reinforced her awareness of how much work there was to do:

> Our first day was all about observation. We walked into the empty kindergarten classroom at the Amelio School. There were maybe forty little plastic chairs in a semi-circle as far away from the teacher's desk as they could possibly be. We watched the teacher come in with her handbag slung over her shoulder and sit down on her chair. The children followed. They were all wearing back-packs and proceeded to sit on their chairs without taking them off. Almost immediately the teacher began to lecture to them. This lasted forty minutes while the children sat silently. Bored, for sure, but totally respectful.
>
> The teacher was not using any resources of any kind. No interchange. No laughter. Not much reaction on either side. After forty minutes the children lined up, went out to play for about twenty minutes, and

came back again. The teacher talked at the children for another forty minutes, then they went out to play for twenty more minutes. This routine was repeated three times until the school day was over.

Kaye Bach handing out hygiene packets; that's Katie Samson with the blond hair in the background.

We knew we needed a systematic plan if we were going to establish a consistent series of teacher training sessions in Siem Reap. To make things more manageable, we decided to start the training at the lower grades and gradually work our way up. This meant beginning with kindergarten teachers.

Because Amelio and Bakong were among the few schools in Cambodia to even have kindergarten classes, we had to create our own kindergarten curriculum, as well as guidance for the teachers. This had a built-in advantage, however. While the lesson plans had to be created from scratch, the curriculum and the teacher training could be developed simultaneously to complement each other. In the eyes of Cambodia's Ministry of Education, since we were breaking new ground by even having a kindergarten class, we had a legitimate reason to train this group of teachers and give them the support they needed to teach. In other words, because there was no status quo, we were no threat and the government did not have to be defensive about our efforts.

The Education Committee spent hundreds of hours preparing for our first formal teachers' training session with the kindergarten teachers, with Kaye, Katie, and Erin taking the lead. They tuned and fine-tuned the training model until they were able to create a manual that not only spelled out specific training techniques, but also underscored the importance of consistency. The manual emphasized that while the curriculum might change, the methods we wanted to use to train the teachers would remain the same. As it turns out, the structure hasn't really changed much over the years.

First we introduce a concept and then we give the teachers the context for teaching it. We then model the concept by teaching it to the teachers, with them in the role of students and us as the teachers. We then flip that model by taking the Cambodian teachers into a classroom, where they observe the trainers teaching actual students.

All the training sessions are translated by simultaneous interpreters recruited by Savy. We are always careful to get buy-in from the Cambodian authorities, and right from the start we brought in government representatives to observe our teacher training sessions.

The Education Committee had decided that the focus of the first kindergarten teacher training session would be math since it did not involve too much language. Kaye, Katie, Liz, and others, including Eleni Scheidt, spent many hours, often on weekends, preparing the lessons and organizing the equipment and resources to take to Siem Reap. They included paints, crayons, shape cutouts, and math manipulatives designed so that students could perceive mathematical concepts by manipulating physical objects. The idea was to give children a way to learn concepts in a hands-on, experiential way.

Kaye describes it more professionally:

> *Our approach was similar to teaching kindergarten in America—circle time and instructional time. We introduced five tabletop activities using math manipulatives to help teach a certain concept—shapes, for example. At five different tables we set up five unique interactive math projects. The idea was to have the children rotate from table to table just like the teachers had in the training session. On one table we might have cardboard cutouts, laminated and hole-punched so the children could follow the shapes by threading the holes with yarn. Another had play dough so the kids could mold geometric shapes with their hands. There was also a table of paints and sponges of different shapes that they used to stamp the shape onto paper. At another table the children had to match plastic colored shapes with the same shapes painted on cardboard.*

We Didn't Know What We Didn't Know

The initial feeling by everyone involved was that this first teacher training session, attended by seven kindergarten teachers from CFC's schools in Bakong and Spien Chrieve and a few from Kravaan, was a huge success. The teachers appeared receptive to the new teaching methods and the kids were almost giddy with new-found engagement. The representatives from Cambodia's Ministry of Education, our toughest critics, also seemed pleased.

Nonetheless, it didn't take us long to realize we had made a number of tactical mistakes. Kaye describes the committee's changing thought process:

Our plan was to show the CFC teachers how to use the manipulatives and other resources and simply hand them over to them. In retrospect, that was completely the wrong way to go. We were living proof that one learns by one's mistakes.

Take the sponge-painting activity, which had unforeseen problems on many fronts. Most of the kindergarten classes had fifty children in them. In Singapore we would never have attempted a paint shape-stamping activity with just one instructor for fifty kids.

In spite of that obvious error, we thought, "We've taught them the concept of using painting to make teaching math more interesting."

That was our second mistake. After we left, sure, they were able to paint on the following Monday. They could even do it again on Tuesday. But by Wednesday, they had run out of paper. We didn't know what we didn't know, in this case that paper was in short supply in Cambodia.

A third problem was the mess it made. The children had no aprons to protect their uniforms, which to the children and their families were like gold. Most of them had just one, possibly two, school outfits, which they wore daily for the entire year. The teachers, rightly so, were totally paranoid about getting the uniforms soiled with paint.

The fourth mistake, the biggest of all, was that here we were coming to Siem Reap for just three days, bringing resources and teaching concepts and expecting these teachers to understand, absorb, and then carry out our vision beyond those five tables of activities. I needed to remind myself of my own "Three Times Rule." After that first session, the teachers were still clueless about how to transfer that kind of creative teaching and learning into other aspects of their curriculum.

This photo reminds me one of our early mistakes—not enough paper for the kids to paint on.

But slowly we had some breakthroughs. The biggest came when Liz was able to get her hands on a full English translation of the Cambodian government's official curriculum, which had just recently been completely overhauled and revamped. It was hard enough to teach the teachers new teaching methods, but to do it during a simultaneous translation of the curriculum was especially difficult. Up until then Savy was doing his best to explain the curriculum to the Education Committee, but it was a tedious process.

Liz remembers this period well:

> We were using the newly adopted National Basic Education curriculum for Cambodian schools, which was supported by USAID and developed by Cambodia's Ministry of Education in partnership with the Research Triangle Institute (RTI). There was one problem, however: it was in the Khmer language. Savy had been translating the documents for us but it was a daunting task given its heavy reliance on educational jargon. But dutifully he would sit down, translate it as best he could, and send it to us.
>
> We knew an English translation existed, but for some reason it was elusive. One day a ministry official gave me the name of the RTI project director who had the documents in English. I emailed him and he sent back a cautionary response, wanting to know how we were intending to use it. Savy stepped in and wrote him a beautiful message, basically saying, "We have your curriculum but we have a group of English-speaking educators who are working with our Cambodian teachers to show them how to use it."

The man wrote back, admitting that Savy was right—
that the translation should be used. Suddenly it appeared
on my email as an attachment and that was that.

This translated curriculum proved to be vital to the development of our teacher training program and ultimately to the successful teaching methods of CFC teachers and administrators.

As we moved through 2006, we continued to rethink, adapt, teach, and be inspired. One practical decision by the Education Committee that made a big difference was to have Katie and Kaye and their teams from their respective schools, Tanglin Trust and SAS, conduct their training sessions at different times during the school year. That way they could reinforce the other's teaching, double the number of teacher training sessions, and train more teachers.

It all stemmed from Kaye's "Three Times Rule" whereby after the third time of teaching the same strategy or technique, teachers would really claim it as their own. We learned a lot from this kindergarten teacher training session and almost immediately started planning for the next one aimed at first grade teachers.

At about this same time, we hired our first full-time staff person, Paige Okun, as chief operating officer, mostly in order to relieve me of some of my administrative burdens. Paige worked for CFC for almost three years and while she and I often clashed, she helped CFC operate more professionally. She also helped identify and define each program we were initiating and taught us how to manage and market them.

I learned a lot from Paige. She was always playing devil's advocate and though I didn't always like it, she was very organized and goal oriented and her steadying influence definitely helped take CFC to another level.

Natalie, Keeper of the Laminator

Back in Singapore the Education Committee continued to create a variety of teaching tools that took into account what we had learned about the practical requirements of the Siem Reap environment.

For example, we had learned that any teaching materials made of paper wilted almost immediately in the incredible Cambodian humidity. The dirty little fingers that were constantly handling the materials didn't help either.

We solved that problem by laminating as many of the teaching supplies as possible. Natalie Bastow, who would become another vital link in CFC's success, created an assembly line of workers to create the materials we needed.

Natalie recalls her own "orange moment" that prompted her commitment to CFC:

> In 2007, after I had been living in Singapore for a year, my husband, who works for UPS, took a business trip to Cambodia. We went there with fellow UPSers, two of whom—Renee and Joe Guerrisi—had made arrangements for us to take paper and pens to CFC schools. Joe had made an earlier visit to Siem Reap with his son's eighth grade SAS class to help in a CFC construction project, but I personally was unaware of CFC's efforts there.
>
> After touring the temples we delivered the supplies we had brought to the Bakong School. We walked around the grounds and observed the classrooms and the teachers. At one point I went over to talk to a little girl who was writing in her notebook. Her Khmer penmanship was remarkably good—perfect, actually.

> *Afterwards I walked out to the center of the school-yard and I don't know, something happened that I know many of us have experienced. I had this overwhelming feeling; now I realize it was a premonition. I've never said this before, but I was standing there thinking that I, that we, could help.*
>
> *My husband came up behind me and he must have seen the look on my face. He knew exactly where I was going. He whispered in my ear, "No, we can't move here."*
> *He knew.*

Natalie, who had been a music teacher in Canada for thirteen years and was now working as a substitute teacher at SAS, didn't move to Siem Reap, but she sure did make a difference, devoting endless hours to various CFC activities. Her first contribution was to organize groups of women in Singapore to get together over coffee, tea, and freshly baked cookies to help create the teaching tools we needed. She called it the "Cut and Paste Club."

Natalie and her team spent hours creating poster boards displaying the letters of the English alphabet next to their colorful corresponding images, like the letter "A" with an apple or the letter "B" with a banana. Other visual aids Natalie's group created included "big books" and "felt boards" large enough so that the children could see them clearly from their eye level during reading and storytelling time.

These women created the "big books" by cutting and pasting colorful images on large pieces of cardboard to illustrate stories. Some of them were store-bought international stories and some were written by our volunteers in Singapore. All of them were translated into the Khmer language.

So that all the materials could withstand the Cambodian heat and the wear and tear of dozens of children, everything had to be laminated, and Natalie began to be referred to as "the keeper of the laminator." Her group was constantly laminating. To take just one example, Natalie and company created an age-appropriate alphabet set for every class. For eight first grade classes they laminated eight sets of poster-size paper for a total of 208 laminations.

CFC teacher and now Director of Administration for all CFC schools, Sarik, in front of laminated letters created in Singapore. A favorite Amelio saying is painted on the wall.

Even so, we continued to underestimate the damage the constant Cambodian heat could cause. To tell the story of "The Three Little Pigs," the Education Committee created felt cutouts of the three pigs, the wolf, and the three houses so the pieces could be moved around as the story was told. Felt is a simple and marvelous teaching tool, but in the stifling Cambodian temperatures it quickly stopped sticking to the boards. The solution was to sew on pieces of Velcro so the cutouts wouldn't slip.

The Education Committee did the same thing with the huge faces it created. Each face sported Velcro where the eyes, nose, mouth, ears, hair, etc. would be, and the kids got to choose a smile, a frown, big ears, small ears, long hair, short hair, and so on to place on the face. They just loved this, and the committee made twenty of these faces with all the corresponding choices.

Natalie, who became chair of the Education Committee when Liz King returned to the United States in the spring of 2008, was also instrumental in making certain the materials we created were culturally relevant. She recalls cleaning the library in one of our schools one day and coming across a picture book in English profiling the hockey player Wayne Gretzky. She turned to one of our early CFC Cambodian staff members, So Sopea, who would later be in charge of our teacher training center and Food for Thought program, and asked if he had ever heard of the "Great One." Not only had he never heard of him, but he had never before seen anyone on skates! In the future Natalie made sure our donations were culturally relevant.

Following the Government's Protocol

As part of our continuing effort to partner with rather than set ourselves apart from the Cambodian educational system, we followed and continue to follow the mission of both Cambodia's Ministry of Education and UNICEF's "Child Friendly Schools" initiative, characterized as "inclusive, healthy and protective for all children, effective . . . and involved with families and communities." This language, which the Cambodian government includes in its curriculum, is wonderful for CFC because it mirrors what we want to do.

According to the UNICEF website, "Schools must not only help children realize their right to basic education of good quality," but also "help children learn what they need to face the challenges of the new century; enhance their health and well-being; and guarantee them safe protective spaces for learning, free from violence and abuse; raise teacher morale and motivation; and mobilize community support for education." We certainly had no argument with any of that!

Each year we also try to use our teacher training materials as a way to complement the teaching themes issued by the Cambodian government and UNICEF. In 2007–'08 the theme was body parts; the next year it was health and hygiene; then reduce, recycle, reuse. In 2010–'11 the theme was respect; this past year it was cooperation.

The Education Committee has had fun adapting its materials to each new topic. When the country-wide focus was on body parts, we developed a lesson plan for the teachers that included having each child lie on top of a large piece of butcher paper. The teacher then drew an outline of the student's body that was subsequently cut out. From there the child added his or her different body parts. This lent itself well to crossing from math, to health/science, to language, to daily life.

Meanwhile, we were slowly learning to hand out materials at teacher training sessions that were sustainable within Siem Reap. Laminated materials brought from Singapore were one thing, but as CFC expanded its reach to additional schools we realized we needed to use materials that could be created and maintained by our CFC staff in Siem Reap. The most obvious early example was that many of the teaching tools we suggested, like the body parts cutout activity, required a substantial amount of paper, yet large quantities of paper were hard to come by in Cambodia at a reasonable price.

Savy solved the problem by finding a local printing company that was throwing away its excess rolls of paper, as well as sheets of thicker paper that we could use as the backing for laminated sheets. We set up a regular schedule for our CFC van to pick up rolls of the unused, unwanted paper, something we still do today. This waste is put to an endless number of uses, including bulletin boards and paper for drawing and painting.

Another time we discovered that the photocopying store we used in Siem Reap was discarding pieces of foam board of varying thickness. We were able to use these for various kinds of displays and white boards. We regularly brought them back to Singapore and drilled holes in them so the kids could sew them together. At first we took everything to Siem Reap in huge duffel bags (we called them body bags) whenever anyone was making a trip, until Natalie created a more organized committee to manage donated goods. Eventually our CFC teachers and staff were able to reproduce most of the materials themselves on site. Today even laminating machines are sold in Siem Reap.

During most teacher training sessions we try to take advantage of being in Siem Reap by having our trainers participate in other events as well. For example, the evening before they return to Singapore we usually host a community meeting at which we distribute either food or hygiene packets or both. Savy usually leads the sessions and he spends most of his time talking about the importance of education. We often coincide the sessions with a MAD or other volunteer trip in order to piggyback on a particular community project. This gets villagers involved, while showing our volunteers the impact they are having on the schools, students, and village. We also introduce the Cambodian teachers to the community, making it clear that these are the men and women who are going to change their children's lives.

All told, working within the guidelines established by the Cambodian government gives us credibility with both the government and the people we most want to assist.

Beautiful children from CFC schools.

Virginia and me in Tuscany, our last trip together.

The stunning Angkor Wat.

Monk in magnificent orange.

Family photo at Angkor Wat's South Gate, one of my favorite spots.

Savy at a temple.

Kravaan classroom before CFC.

Jade Ausley and Mary Beth Shay with CFC caring HANDS.

The school in the village of Spien Chrieve where Savy taught English. It was here that CFC built the Amelio School, our first school.

Traditional dance at the Amelio school opening. October 24, 2003. Rathana is on the far right, and Manoot on the far left.

Bright and cheery CFC classroom. Please note Pen Rithy's fabulous mural (background left), and the brilliant Cambodian-made bulletin boards enriching the classroom with color and fun learning.

Make a Difference (MAD) trip, 2004.

Ribbon cutting ceremony at Kong Much. Austin to my right, Savy to the left. Bill and Riley looking on from behind.

Chea Sophea and Vandy, two mentor teachers, with Katie Samson, master teacher trainer.

Vandy teaching a lesson with felt. A student Star of the Week with her crown is sitting in the first row.

SAS 8th grade and teacher training trip to Siem Reap.

Wheelbarrow fun with SAS teacher trainers and CFC students.

A newly constructed playground at the Aranh school.

House-building by volunteers working side-by-side with Cambodians.

Jen and me; the Amelios are standing nearby.

A completed house built by CFC volunteers on stilts.

CFC Board of Directors trip, 2007. (l-r) Chok Dary, Mum, Marybeth Shay, me, Paige Okun, Sandra Smith, Savy, Christy Miller, Karen Deberry, Lori Mconaghy, Eleni Scheidt, Liz King, and Samedi.

SIX

More Than Reading, Writing, and Arithmetic

For the 2005 school year the suggested area of focus from Cambodia's Ministry of Education was health and hygiene. In Cambodia, as we knew all too well, health and hygiene is much more than a slogan; it is a life and death issue for many, many Cambodian children.

During the first year the Amelio School was open we lost children to malnutrition, dental infections, dysentery, and dengue fever. Beyond that, chronic diarrhea, worms, and intestinal parasites caused extraordinarily high absenteeism. While teaching our kids reading, writing, and arithmetic was important to give them a start at a well-rounded education, they clearly needed our help in more profound and practical ways, too.

Health and hygiene thus became a vital part of our curriculum and teacher training. We started with the basics, like teaching kids to wash their hands before eating and brushing their teeth. In Cambodia, this is the kind of knowledge that can save lives.

Kong Much seconder grader in need of dental care.

We formalized our emphasis on health and hygiene into what we call our Bright Smiles Bright Futures program, which promotes overall good health and a sense of worth by requiring our younger students to brush their teeth after every in-school meal. For families in Siem Reap, where toothbrushes are a luxury, we now make sure every student receives three new ones each school year.

Since 2005 we've received donations of tens of thousands of toothbrushes from children across the globe, everywhere from Singapore to Australia to Washington, DC, where during Halloween youngsters collect new toothbrushes for us along with trick or treating for candy. Thousands more toothbrushes come from doctors and dentists in Singapore and from teachers and student volunteers in schools and communities around the world.

Something as simple as brushing their teeth has had a remarkable impact on our students' health and their lives. We see it every day. Most CFC classrooms now have a hygiene corner where every child keeps a toothbrush and a cup for clean drinking water. Teachers oversee the brushing of teeth once a day as part of a discussion of the science of dental hygiene and the ramifications of not brushing their teeth.

We have also made dental hygiene an important part of our teacher training curriculum. During the 2009 mid-term break, for example, nine teachers from the Tanglin Trust School, headed by Katie Sansom, came to Siem Reap and introduced a number of health initiatives to third and fourth grade teachers, leaving behind a series of lesson plans, follow-up activities, and dental supply kits, all focused on the importance of good hygiene.

Clean Classrooms

Our focus on health and hygiene also provided the perfect opportunity to teach the concept of cleanliness, both in body and in the environment. At schools across Cambodia time is reserved each Thursday to sweep and clean the classrooms, but as I mentioned earlier, every day is cleanup day at CFC schools. Our teacher training program planted the seeds to get the teachers thinking about how great it would feel to have no dust on Tuesdays, no mud on Wednesdays, and a clean classroom when school resumed on Monday morning.

We often threw out concepts like this and then watched the Cambodian teachers come up with their own solutions. Such a process is always exciting, and teachers are filled with great pride when their ideas are successful.

Today not a day goes by when you don't see children and faculty involved in keeping their school's classrooms and grounds, including the flower and vegetable gardens, neat and tidy.

Nevertheless, a continuing challenge for CFC is determining what our teachers know and don't know given their own life experiences. Our discussions with them about health, hygiene, and classroom cleanliness only resonate with them, and ultimately with their students, if we can get into their heads and see problems from their perspective.

One day Savy mentioned to one of our third grade teachers that his classroom was particularly dirty and disorganized and asked him to have his students help him clean it. The next day as the teacher was leaving school he reported that he had done what he had been asked and that his classroom was now clean.

When Savy walked in to take a look he found dust everywhere and rubbish still on the tables and floor. Savy was really angry, something you don't see very often, but a few days later he gained some insight into the situation when he attended the wedding of this teacher's daughter. What Savy saw in the man's home opened his eyes. Even on this most important day his house was a mess—dusty and dirty, with clutter everywhere. This man did not know what clean was, so how was he supposed to set an example for the kids in his classroom?

This was another reminder that our teachers needed to be taught not just how to be teachers, but how to be good citizens. This included everything from their own hygiene to how reading a newspaper could help them stay current about Cambodia and the rest of world.

We had come a long way in terms of getting our teachers to feel proud of their role in the community as teachers, but many of them still did not know how to take full responsibility or have high expectations for themselves. In addition to giving them teaching skills and resources, our teacher training sessions were about getting them to understand the tremendous opportunities and responsibilities their jobs entailed.

Extending Our Teaching beyond School Walls

Another gradual realization was that if we were truly going to make a difference in the lives of the young children attending CFC schools, our most basic lessons about health and hygiene needed to be reinforced at home. We had to revolutionize Cambodian thinking and make parents understand that *normal* could be something other than children with diarrhea, lice, and pink eye. We had to explain to them the ramifications of bathing, drinking, and relieving themselves in the same riverbed. We had to show them what a healthy child looked like and then teach them what could be done to keep them that way by emphasizing lessons in school that the children could take home and share.

Consequently, we made talking to parents about oral hygiene part of our students' required homework. We wanted our kids to go home healthy, but also to tell their parents what they had done at school that day, including brushing their teeth and sweeping their classrooms to keep out the dust and dirt.

CFC also began reinforcing this message at community outreach events called "Hygiene in the Home" where we serve healthy meals as a motivating force to get as many people as possible to attend. Then we distribute hygiene packages containing soap, a comb, a toothbrush, and toothpaste.

These health and hygiene initiatives have been enormously successful, and I dare say you can tell just by looking at CFC kids that they are healthier than the children who attend non-CFC schools. We can only hope they will use these skills for the rest of their lives and pass them on to their own children.

Food for Thought

Encouraging CFC students to brush their teeth and to keep themselves and their environment clean was a start, but we faced an even bigger problem when we realized that many of our children were arriving at school hungry.

Home visits revealed that some children not only routinely ate no breakfast, but that sometimes they went a day or more with almost no food at all. The piece of candy or bread a friend might give them at school might be all they ate during the entire school day.

I was so naïve those first months that I actually thought a swollen belly meant a child had a full stomach. The reality was that some of our children were starving. We had to do something about this. Learning under these conditions was impossible. This also helped to explain our continuing problem with chronic absenteeism and why our part-time nurse was overwhelmed with the number of children who always seemed to be ill with one ailment or another.

The solution became obvious to Savy and to those of us working on the problem back in Singapore: if we wanted our children to learn on full stomachs, we were going to have to feed them ourselves.

We started small (bird by bird) by serving breakfast informally under the trees on the Amelio School campus. We paid a few mothers from the village to buy vegetables, fruits, and rice, either from the market or from village stands, and when they returned with the food and receipts, other CFC volunteers and local moms prepared the food and served it to the kids.

We called this program Food for Thought and it was an instant success. I swear that within days I could see a difference in the kids. They looked healthier, more energetic, more interested, and happier, and it was clear we had to expand the program to our other schools as quickly as we could find the funds. At the same time, we did a gut check to make sure we weren't straying from our goal of providing a free, quality education.

In order to stay focused, one of our early tenets required us to concentrate on what Bill called "the critical few versus the trivial many." His point was that in any initiative we undertook we had to make certain we were not being diverted from our primary goal of providing a better education to the students in our schools. Therefore, before we took on any task, we scrutinized it to make sure it did not lead us astray.

In this case we asked ourselves if in addition to educating kids about the importance of good nutrition, actually feeding them every day was the right thing to do. After all, a substantial amount of funding and focus would be needed to support an expansion of Food for Thought into every one of our schools. But I knew we had to do it. Kids were starving when they arrived at school and clearly they could not learn if they were not fed.

We went through a similar process with teacher training. The lynchpin of CFC is the idea that the best way to move people through the educational process is through great teachers. We can all remember a teacher who touched us, someone who made an enormous difference in our lives. We also understood the importance of having great teachers in Cambodia and that the previous generation of teachers had been wiped out by the Khmer Rouge. It seemed logical to us to make the training of teachers central to our mission.

Just like the formalization of our teacher training program, Food for Thought was another huge turning point for CFC and we jumped into it wholeheartedly. We knew we would need to create a real cafeteria with real cooks and a real infrastructure and find someone in Cambodia to run the day-to-day operation of providing a healthy breakfast for every CFC student. As usual, we found just the person we were looking for through a bit of serendipity, combined with some typical Savy magic.

By this time, our MAD trips were regularly building homes for the neediest families living in our school districts. Savy had a real knack for finding those who could use our help the most, and in early 2005 he had identified a grandmother named Jen who was living in a termite-infested home near the Amelio School. Like most of the homes in the village, hers was built on stilts of wood and palm leaf roots, but as you walked inside your feet would break through chunks of the wood floor that then fell to the ground below. The house had become so unstable that Jen's daughter and grandchildren had gone to live with an aunt in another province and her son and other grandkids had had to find somewhere else to live as well. Jen was still living there, now all alone.

Savy knew Jen was in danger with no source of income or any family to lean on when he suggested we build her a house. During one of CFC's volunteer trips, I think it was a corporate team-building event, a group of CFC volunteers did just that.

On my first visit back to Cambodia after Jen's house was built I went right from the airport to visit her in her new home. She was once again living there with her extended family, including her grandkids who were now able to return to the Amelio School.

As soon as she saw me Jen held her hands together as if in prayer and dropped to her knees, bowing and crying profusely with gratitude, practically begging Savy and me to find a way she could repay us.

I started crying too, deeply moved and humbled. Cambodian protocol is very reserved and people generally do not touch each other. Jen's traditional yet exuberant expression of thanks was so moving that I picked her up and gave her a huge hug.

The next day Savy explained the Food for Thought program and asked Jen if she would become our chief cook. *Never let a good deed go to waste*, I thought.

Jen did not have to be asked twice. "Absolutely yes," she told us. "This is how I will repay my debt to you. I will work for the school forever."

Five days a week Jen rises at 4:30 a.m. to be at the Amelio School by 5:00 a.m. in order to prepare breakfast for the children, who arrive at 6:00.

A typical breakfast consists of vegetables, rice or porridge served with wonderful Cambodian spices like lemongrass or tarot root, and some kind of meat or fish.

Today our Food for Thought program feeds 6,400 children (a number that seems to increase every day) at our sixteen CFC schools. It is a beautiful thing to see, a stark contrast to the noise and clatter of school cafeterias in the United States. CFC students come with their bowls in hand and are served by volunteers, at which point they bow with gratitude and thanks. They return to their tables where they eat in almost total silence, treating the meal with quiet respect and serenity. Afterwards they go to the sink to clean their bowls and utensils and to brush their teeth. Visitors and volunteers often tell me that serving the children breakfast is their most memorable experience in Cambodia.

We buy only locally produced food, most of it grown in the villages surrounding each of the schools, so our Food for Thought program benefits the entire community. Volunteers, usually the parents and grandparents of CFC schoolchildren, buy the staples we need from village markets or from the old market in Siem Reap and then cook and prepare the meals.

Eventually our goal is to have more and more of the vegetables we serve come from gardens on our campuses that our students help cultivate. In the meantime, we've added fish ponds on some of our campuses that provide fish for the children to eat at mealtimes and that teach them how to reproduce these sustainable farms at home.

The entire Food for Thought operation is coordinated by a young man named So Sopea, a former student at the Amelio School. According to Savy, So Sopea was "heading down the wrong path," but his involvement with CFC "straightened him out." Sopea has become a responsible and dutiful contributor to CFC and his community and I expect he is a future leader of CFC.

Food for Thought has been so successful that in February of 2011 we made the decision to expand it to two meals a day. Our kids may have been eating breakfast, but they still weren't eating enough, as evidenced by their skinny frames, and I knew we could do more.

Many times since I started CFC I made snap decisions based on what I knew in my heart was right despite what anyone else said and this was one of those times. Savy initially gulped but he made it happen, and by the first of April in 2011 lunches, too, were being served in all our schools. We even feed the hungry siblings of our students, younger brothers and sisters who are too little to go to school but who are just as hungry. We don't turn any child away.

Our annual budget for Food for Thought is about $70,000 (less than $1 per child per day) and is available thanks in part to another "orange" moment. In February of 2005 Liz King's friend Blair Speciale visited Siem Reap for the first time. For many months Blair worked in the background, participating in MAD trips and helping to clean and stock the libraries. She started bringing her family on some of her visits, including her husband Mark, who at the time worked for the Capital Group Companies. Mark became hooked too, and Capital Group has been making a generous annual donation to our Food for Thought program ever since.

We raise additional funds for Food for Thought through a number of fundraising events in Singapore, including our annual Easter Egg-a-thon. Last year more than two hundred people searched for about three thousand eggs that they collected in handmade Cambodian baskets. The event includes a dunk tank, raffle tickets, a silent auction, and refreshments. In its first few years the Egg-a-thon was held at the home of Raju and Steve Shaulis, but it grew to the point that we had to move it to a local soccer field. As always, this event is made possible by a group of volunteers. People like Erin Isernhagen pour their hearts and souls into making it a fantastic day for everyone who attends, knowing all the while the proceeds will benefit the kids who attend our CFC schools.

Kong Much

After the opening of the school in Bakong we were all crazy busy trying to make constant improvements at both our CFC schools and to rev up our Food for Thought and teacher training initiatives. Starting a third school was the furthest thing from my mind, but not from Savy's. In early 2005 he suggested that he and I drop by the school in the village of Kong Much, located just down the road from Spien Chrieve. He knew some of the teachers and families there and they had approached him to see if we could do the same thing in Kong Much that we had done in Spien Chrieve and Bakong.

I was interested. The Amelio School was already overflowing with students and some of them came from outside Spien Chrieve in neighboring villages, including Kong Much. A growing recognition that CFC schools were special meant that more and more parents wanted their children to attend one of our schools rather than the school closest to them.

Kong Much was a challenge right from the start but I couldn't say no. We had done it in Spien Chrieve and we could do it in Kong Much, but this time we had to virtually tear down the entire campus. Termites had almost completely eaten through the main building and the air inside the classroom was filled with a thick, I'm sure unhealthy, dust. The grounds were littered with trash and the smell was like being on the outskirts of a garbage dump. Still, I remember standing at the edge of the campus with Susan Mars, a good friend and at the time a neighbor in Singapore, and concluding that it was a great site with tons of potential. It sat next to a beautiful monastery and it felt right.

It took us five months to rebuild the Kong Much School from the ground up, three buildings at once. One building was a gift from Frank DeJong, an executive at Emerson Process Management Asia, in memory of his wife Allison, one of our earliest supporters who had passed away a few months earlier. This contribution made our adoption of the Kong Much School possible and I always think of Allison whenever I enter that building.

Kong Much School now has fifteen classrooms, a library, and a computer lab, and a team of CFC volunteers recently added a playground, but back then Kong Much had deeper problems than our schools in either Spien Chrieve or Bakong. Somehow the energy was different, starting with the principal, who was often nowhere to be found for days on end. Taking that as their cue, many of the teachers were regularly absent. In addition, their teaching methods were rigidly chalk and talk, and few of them were interested in teaching any differently. Most of the teachers at Bakong and Amelio had jumped at the chance to participate in teacher training, but we literally had to bribe the teachers at Kong Much to attend.

During our first few months there we even started experiencing nighttime break-ins and the regular disappearance of school supplies. Perhaps the burglaries were due to the school's proximity to the main road and vulnerability to strangers, or maybe a group of malcontent teachers were responsible. After all, we were making changes to the status quo very quickly.

By early 2006, a few months after the new school opened, the situation had gotten so bad that Savy appealed to Kong Much's village elders. He told them that if the villagers did not respect their school and did not want to accept our help, then CFC was going to pull out. We were serious, and the situation began to improve. The community started to keep a careful lookout, and the break-ins stopped.

At the same time, our teacher training sessions, health and hygiene initiatives, and Food for Thought program gradually began to take hold.

We were also given a new principal, which also made a huge difference. Kong Much is now one of our proudest achievements, with enrollment in grades K–6 at about 640 students, more than double than when it opened.

Another Year, Enormous Strides

By the end of the 2005–'06 school year we had made considerable strides. We had three schools up and running and we had a cadre of volunteers in Singapore and an increasing number in the United States. We also had a growing staff of employees in Cambodia.

Most importantly, we were beginning to see big changes at the schools. Each morning and then again in the afternoon the children in their clean uniforms would line up on the school grounds and pledge their allegiance to the Cambodian flag, then sing the national anthem. At the end of each school day they would stand with a backpack slung over their shoulders as one of the teachers or student council members reinforced what they had learned that day and addressed any problems that might have developed.

Student Council members.

At the Bakong School we also had a new group of adult learners, a few older monks from the Bakong Monastery who unexpectedly came to school one day. At first we thought they were former teachers who wanted their jobs back, but then we realized they had come because they too were hungry to learn.

By year's end we had teachers who were being trained, kids who were being fed, and monks who were learning on the computer and being taught English. Particularly for the older monks, learning in this modern way filled a huge gap in their lives. Their humble presence behind computers presented a snapshot of how Cambodia was moving from its dark, horrific past into a more modern, more hopeful present. In order for the children, the teachers, and even the monks to know there could be a better way, they needed to see something different. That's what we were trying to do, and it was working. We could see that it was really working.

The stakes at this point were high and failure was not an option. I frequently struggled with how to be a better leader, with how to get more people involved to take on different jobs, and most importantly, with how to follow-up on our successes. I also engaged in a lot of "self talk" during these years as I learned how to step back and not micromanage. This was particularly true of my involvement with the Education Committee, which was filled with women much more knowledgeable than I about early childhood education.

Bill's advice and guidance during these months helped me understand that good leaders create a situation in which other people can succeed, and that was the gauge I eventually learned to use. If the volunteers felt like they were getting things done, we would be successful. After all, I wanted CFC to be the volunteers' organization, not Jamie Amelio's. Although I was regularly in touch with the Education Committee's chair, these amazing educators were the ones who laid the foundation for the success and growth of the entire CFC organization.

SEVEN

Rathana and Cherry

Sometimes I think the idea of having two Cambodian children come live with us in Singapore originated the day in 2003 when I visited Siem Reap for the first time. But really the idea grew slowly, as the children and the communities within the CFC school districts began to feel like extensions of my own family.

I met Rathana for the first time during one of my early visits to Spien Chrieve. At this point the school was just one concrete building alongside a bamboo hut made of palm leaves. As Savy and I drove up I saw a little girl sitting on a bench by herself, absentmindedly rolling a few small stones around in her hand. It must have been lunchtime, or just after school had let out, because there was no one else in sight. Curious, I walked in her direction and stopped to ask her name.

"Rathana," she told me, breaking into a grin. "I am nine," she added, holding up nine fingers.

We sat together on the cracked cement bench talking in Rathana's broken English and my infantile Khmer, with Savy weighing in to translate when necessary.

Much later Rathana told me she remembers our first meeting slightly differently:

> *My first memory of seeing my mom, she was with Bronson and they were handing me a yellow and red backpack as a gift. Goodbye to my plastic bag. My first impression was of her smile, and that she wanted to be connected to the children. Not just "Here is a backpack," but asking me my name, what I was interested in, how old I was. She made me want to reach out to her, to tell her my stories.*

As Rathana told me her stories during the weeks and month that followed, I couldn't get her out of my mind. To me she became the face of CFC. She was the face I remembered and in fact literally dreamt about. She symbolized all my hopes—the beautiful little girl with rotting teeth, long hair, big smile, and constant questions.

On every subsequent visit to Siem Reap I spent time with Rathana, usually either at lunch or right after school. It became our little thing to practice English together. She was never shy with me; she clung to me in a way that was different from any of the other children. We had our own way of communicating, with me teaching her English words, usually without the need for an interpreter, while she taught me what it was like to be nine, then ten, then eleven years old in Cambodia.

Rathana in 2004. Oh that quiet smile!

During one early visit Rathana handed me a few drawings she had made. After that, each time I saw her she would carefully lift new ones from a small envelope and give them to me. Her drawings were of what she saw around the school and her home, mostly flowers and trees. She had never been anywhere else. She told me about wanting to be an artist and I tried to convey to her what that meant in the big world outside of Siem Reap. I wondered if she knew what an artist really was. Actually, I knew she didn't know. But dreams are important, and I desperately wanted them to be part of her life.

Rathana was intensely curious about where I came from and how I lived, but also about why I kept coming back to Cambodia. I was just as curious about her life, but also about what she thought about the future. As she began to trust that I would keep returning we developed a strong bond until one day she invited me to meet her family.

Rathana's house was right off the road, and while it had a large porch, strong walls, and more land than the typical village home, even during my first couple of visits I could see that her family life was less than ideal. An extraordinary number of family members were living under the same roof, grandmas and aunts and uncles and cousins, many of them constantly arriving and departing. Although the new Cambodian Constitution had outlawed polygamy, Rathana's father had another wife and family living nearby. With Rathana's mom he had five children; Rathana was right in the middle.

This was one of those families where in spite of some difficult family dynamics, the children had a creative spark. One of Rathana's older brothers, Pen Rithy, had some serious issues with his father and sometimes he and the other children stayed next door with their grandmother. Rithy nonetheless became an accomplished artist. He is the one who painted the murals in the Amelio School's classrooms. One of our real success stories, he currently attends the Royal University in Phnom Penh. Another brother, Pen Ratha, is a talented dancer and recently graduated from culinary school in Siem Reap.

About a year after I began spending time with Rathana, visiting with her nearly every time I traveled to Siem Reap, she introduced me to her best friend Cherry, another Amelio School student who lived just across the road. Unlike the gregarious Rathana, Cherry would hide in the classroom when I visited, although one day I noticed her sitting alone at a desk, an image that is immortalized in one of our brochures.

Cherry always seemed to be barefoot, even when riding to school on her bicycle, her tiny feet struggling to reach the pedals. She had to stand up straight and push one pedal down, then the other, her short legs in constant motion.

Cherry has her own memory of those first days of our getting to know each other:

> *The first time I met my mom she just came up to me and asked my name. I was a little bit shy. I was the girl who was quiet and wasn't really involved when all the American people came and helped with all the buildings.*
>
> *Then she just came to me and introduced herself and I was a little bit like, "Okay, she just came to me, yeah!" I don't know what she's saying, I just know that she asks my name, and I say, "Cher-i-ya." And she says, "Okay, but I can't really pronounce it!" She was figuring out what she should call me, and she said, "Well, I give you the nickname Cherry!" And I was like, "Okay! My nickname is Cherry now!"*

Cherry (in the foreground) with 2nd grade friends.

Gradually Cherry too opened up to me. As my friend Christy Miller said when she first met her, she was like "a budding flower—sweet, always blooming."

Cherry's mom was not educated, having spent her formative years working in the fields during the Khmer Rouge rule, but she was very involved in raising her children and Cherry had a stable and caring family life. She grew up with her parents, brother, and maternal grandfather, who in 2006 sold some land and used the proceeds to build a new family home. Her dad, Savin, is a nurse, which in their village means everyone comes to him with their ailments 24/7. Early on he became CFC's full-time nurse so I have gotten to know him well over the years.

On one MAD trip I sent five-year-old Bronson off to play with Rathana and Cherry and Rathana's older brothers while the rest of us borrowed CFC bicycles and rode around the village visiting a number of families whose students attended, or perhaps should have been attending, our school. At the end of the day Bronson and the others met us back at the school and I asked him what they had been doing.

"We were at Cherry's house looking at the crocodiles," he told me.

"Oh, sure," I said. Bronson has always had a good imagination.

"Mom, Cherry has pet crocodiles," he insisted.

Yeah, and I'm an astronaut, I thought, but then the other kids started talking about the crocodiles and I decided I had better see for myself.

We drove in the CFC van to Cherry's house and I almost passed out. In her backyard was a huge manmade pool with a lookout platform from which you could watch what appeared to be dozens of crocodiles. Cherry's dad had the idea he could breed the gators for skins to be turned into shoes, belts, and purses to sell in tourist shops. That never worked out particularly well, although Savin did have some success selling the babies.

The pool also became a kind of tourist attraction. People liked to throw snakes in and watch the crocodiles eat them, often in one gulp.

Another fan favorite was watching Cherry's grandfather walk into the water up to his waist and poke at the crocodiles, some more than eight feet long, with a long pole.

Needless to say, after seeing the gators for myself I didn't allow Bronson to go to Cherry's again without me.

Cherry's Story

Rathana, Cherry, and I became a threesome, meeting every time I visited Siem Reap, usually at the Amelio School, where we'd sit and talk and read together. We talked about school and what they were learning, but also about their hopes and dreams for the future. Slowly I learned that even their lack of any concept of looking forward to a better life was deeply rooted in the past. After all, how could people who had learned in their own childhoods to distrust their neighbors pass on the concept of hope to their children? Their future, indeed their very lives, had been at the whim of the man standing next to them with an axe or a gun.

Years went by before I learned the details of Rathana's and Cherry's families' stories during the Khmer Rouge years. Some of what I learned came from a ninth grade school paper Cherry wrote that also laid out the facts about the Khmer Rouge rule, about how Pol Pot had killed over two million Cambodians, including most of the educated people after deciding that only the educated would have the power to unite against him.

Cherry noted that 75 percent of the country's more than 20,000 teachers were killed and that only 50 out of 725 university instructors, 207 of 2,300 secondary schoolteachers, and 2,727 of 21,311 primary school teachers survived. But the most powerful passages in her paper were about her own family, particularly her grandfather, whom she described as "a great man, a survivor."

Cherry has given me permission to share a few excerpts:

My grandfather told me that Pol Pot killed people who wore glasses because he thought glasses signified you were smart and educated.

In 1975 my grandfather experienced first-hand the cruelty of the Khmer Rouge. Remembering what happened when they entered his village, he told me, "I was scared; I didn't know what to do; I just grabbed my wife and my seven-year-old daughter. I still remember the sounds of the big bomb [gun fire]. We ran as fast as we could but they still caught us."

On another occasion he told me how difficult life was. "They made us work every single day with very little rest. Sometimes they told us to dig dirt and carry heavy stuff. If we were lazy or disobeyed their orders they would punish us; many around me were killed. We were given very little to eat; I was hungry all the time."

My grandfather also told me that when he was starving he would go looking for food. Oftentimes he would eat banana leaves and grass to survive. He did everything he could to stay alive for his family. When the Khmer Rouge regime came into power it continued the devastation by destroying education and religion and turning the country's economy and Cambodian culture and civilization back to "Year Zero."

In order to reach this perfect society, all citizens would have to live as peasants. Modern ideas were considered evil and anyone who was educated posed a threat. With this in mind, Pol Pot began rounding up monks, artists, and intellectuals. Teachers were executed, schools were closed, books were burned, and people were forbidden to read.

The Khmer Rouge's reign of terror ended in 1979. Throughout the country children lived on the streets, begging for money to buy food because their parents couldn't afford to feed them. The people had nothing - no food, no clothes, and no education.

Cherry then goes on to describe herself:

I was born in Cambodia and lived there until I was eleven years old. Some of my friends rarely went to school and others never went. When I asked them why, they would say that their mothers made them find jobs to help with the family finances. Most of the children would sell vegetables or fish at the market. All those children wanted to go to school so badly. I could see it in their eyes but they couldn't do anything about it. Many of their parents were uneducated and resigned to a life of poverty. Having a few dollars to buy food and the other bare necessities was more important than their children attending school. In order to survive, everyone had to work. Their lives were ruined and now they were ruining their children's lives. It was not their fault; it was because of the Khmer Rouge's devastation and destruction.

Today Cambodia is still trying to figure things out. It is slowly making progress but still needs more time to undo the years of turmoil brought on by the Khmer Rouge.

Cherry had never before asked her family about their experiences during the Khmer Rouge years and the writing assignment allowed her to confront that era herself for the first time.

Rathana Visits Singapore

For as long as I had known Rathana she had been part of a children's troupe that performed traditional Cambodian dances for tour groups, primarily on Sunday evenings. She and her brother were both stunning dancers, magnificent and precise, and it occurred to me that SAS's annual spring cultural festival offered the perfect opportunity to have her and other dancers come to Singapore for a visit.

I still had not shared with anyone my thoughts about having Rathana spend some time with us in Singapore. I'm not sure I had even admitted it to myself. I did think that a visit by the dance troupe would call attention within the Singapore expat community to the children of Cambodia and at the same time give these kids an experience they would never forget.

The idea was met with immediate enthusiasm in both Singapore and Siem Reap. Once the plan began to develop the outpouring of support in Singapore surprised me and I think it helped propel CFC forward during what were still our formative years. I know that our small but growing community of CFC volunteers and supporters were moved when they thought of the impact a visit would have on the members of the troupe. Particularly those who had already visited Siem Reap and seen the primitive conditions in which these children lived understood the emotion of the event and became passionate about making it happen.

The hurdles were considerable, starting with getting the children passports and immunized, not an easy task given that they had neither birth certificates nor medical records. We also had to arrange for Cambodian chaperones and get them too through customs without a hitch. The support of the SAS community was critical in making the practical preparations to ensure the visit itself went smoothly and in assuring both governments that we could pull this off safely and without any diplomatic snafus.

The SAS Arts Council paid for new costumes to replace the troupe's old, tattered ones. SAS families offered their homes so the dancers would have a place to stay. A buddy system was created so that each Cambodian child would have a Singapore counterpart to accompany them everywhere they went.

As for the children themselves, they were giddy in anticipation of visiting what might as well have been a different planet. Complicating our efforts, however, was the fact that dancing, even traditional Cambodian dance, had a negative connotation in many families, particularly for girls.

"In Cambodia that's not something they want the girls to do," explains Rathana. "I was going against tradition, but I wanted to dance. That's what I wanted to do. And I felt very proud dancing in front of Americans and Singaporeans. Coming as a dancer, I was excited and nervous with stage fright. But dancing for people who really appreciate your tradition and sharing what you know about your country and showing it to the world made me feel proud as a Cambodian."

In March of 2005 fourteen Cambodian dancers plus a few extra children to help out arrived for a three-day visit. Those of us fortunate to be involved had a front row seat at a classic fish-out-of-water drama as we watched these children enter a world they had never even imagined. Everything was novel and enchanting to them. None of them had ever been on an airplane before. They had never been on an escalator, ridden in an automobile, or seen a modern kitchen. I think what astonished them most was the hot water that flowed out of the taps. Many of them kept turning the water off and on as if they were personally performing an act of legerdemain. Nothing went unnoticed, for them or for us.

That included the lice. Lori McConaghy, one of our early CFC volunteers, had taken most of the dance troupe to visit a department store (something else they marveled at) and noticed lice crawling out of one of the girl's hair. This was an ongoing problem that freaked out some of the Singapore families, but at our house we just got into the habit of having the kids wash their hair with a special shampoo, always and often. I made my own kids use it too.

The day of the performance was magical. The SAS' proscenium theater, like much of Singapore's architecture, is vast and modern, akin to what you might find on a university campus in the United States. The lights slowly dimmed and out of the darkness Cambodian music began to play. Suddenly spotlights revealed fourteen starry-eyed children in perfect makeup and glittering gold costumes dancing precisely to the hypnotic melody. All those kids . . . nervous, carsick, terrified, and yet stunningly beautiful, were poised to perfection.

Rathana and her brother stayed in our home along with three other adorable girls. None of them spoke English but they all got along great with my four children. When you are ten years old you are able to communicate in different ways. I'm sure the idea that one of them might become a nagging sister never crossed the minds of the Amelio children, but during this first trip it certainly crossed mine.

For Rathana and the other dancers the experience was one they would never forget.

"I thought I was dreaming," Rathana remembers. "When I woke up I said to my friends, 'Pinch me. Pinch me. Tell me this is actually true!' I couldn't believe that yesterday I was in Cambodia and today I am in Singapore. How did this happen?"

Sometimes, looking back, I feel the same way.

Rathana and Cherry
Join Our Family

After the dance troupe's visit my routine returned to normal, which for me meant visiting Siem Reap once a month or so in order to continue improving the schools we had opened and to turn our sights toward opening others. I also began talking privately with a handful of CFC members about the idea of bringing a few Cambodian children to Singapore for an extended stay, not through a formal adoption, but as a way to help them through elementary and secondary school and perhaps even college. Together, a handful of us imagined what it would mean both for them and for our own families.

Meanwhile, I continued to get to know Rathana and Cherry better, although communicating between visits was difficult. Neither of their homes had Internet access, although I did occasionally send them short notes by regular mail, usually just to tell them about my next trip to Siem Reap.

On one visit I was horrified to learn that Rathana had spent nine days in the hospital with a tooth abscess. She had become extremely sick, with the entire left side of her face paralyzed, until the antibiotics finally kicked in.

Rathana told me she had spent most of her time on a cot in a room with thirty other sick children, including a number of constantly crying infants. I was frightened to think of Rathana or Cherry spending their teenage years in this environment, and it was definitely a motivating factor in taking my idea a step further.

I hadn't yet said anything to Bill about inviting a Cambodian child into our lives, much less both Rathana *and* Cherry. I was still getting my own mind around what it would mean for Bill and me and for our kids.

But as usual, Bill knew what I was thinking. Although we hadn't yet addressed the issue head on, he had given me plenty of hints that he wasn't exactly wild about the idea of adding to our already big, boisterous family. He would see my reaction after visiting a hospital where parents had abandoned their children, or hear me comment about how adorable a little girl or baby was, and he'd say, "Don't ask. Don't ask."

"All right, all right," I would respond, but my acquiescence was probably not entirely convincing.

I wanted to choose just the right moment to broach the subject with Bill. The opportunity came when he had to be in Hong Kong on a business trip that coincided with our wedding anniversary. I flew there to meet him for a romantic weekend on a scorching spring day in that intensely urbanized city-state. My news, I knew, was going to add to the heat, but I figured I would drop the bomb after a bottle of wine at dinner. In hindsight it wasn't really a bomb; it was more like an ambush.

We shed some tears that night, but in the end we were on the same page, together deciding to invite Rathana and Cherry into our lives. Of the words we said a few flash in my memory: a commitment to raise them together and raise them well; thinking outside the box; being blessed and wanting to share our good fortune with others; and truly believing this was the right thing to do.

Bill's version more or less parallels mine:

> *Our fourth child had just been born when Jamie said to me, "I really like kids!" I said, "I like kids too, so let's have a lot more!" But she said, "No, no, I think I would like to have a child from Cambodia." I thought for a while, then asked if she was serious. "Yes," she was serious.*
>
> *I didn't even think we could legally adopt a child from Cambodia, particularly an older child, and I wondered how we would even bring a child over to Singapore.*

But Jamie had already come up with the idea of a guardianship. She told me that others in the Singapore community were interested too, and she suggested we bring over a few girls and see how it worked out. One would live with us, some with others.

Well, it didn't work out exactly like that. Jamie returned from Siem Reap one day and said to me, "I can't make up my mind. There are these two girls I have really fallen in love with. They're great girls and they have great families over there and we could have them both come live with us."

"Whoa, whoa, whoa, whoa," I said. "Stop for a minute. We went from zero to now two. This is not like a buddy system. Why two?" But just like Jamie, she told me it was all going to work out and she was right. We ended up with two blessings in our life.

The decision did not end there, of course. This was a family matter, so when Bill was home next we called a family meeting to discuss the idea with our kids. We asked for their opinions, starting from the youngest to the oldest, although we all decided that Avery did not get a vote since she was only a baby, not even walking or talking yet.

Bronson was in kindergarten. CFC had always been a big part of his life, so to him this seemed like a natural step. He said "Sure!" right off the bat.

Riley was in the fourth grade, just a few months younger than Cherry, and he simply said, "Fine, whatever."

Austin, although he had just left Singapore for college, loved the energy the girls brought into our home and gave the idea "a strong thumbs up."

It was unanimous.

By this time I knew my idea to have Rathana and Cherry come live with us for a while would not come as a total shock to either girls' parents, but first I wanted to make sure they would be accepted by SAS. This was only going to work if all the children in the Amelio household attended the same school, which meant SAS needed to understand and accept the challenge we were presenting them with. After all, there was no precedent for this. The girls knew very little English, and surely they wouldn't be academically equal to the other SAS students their age.

To his credit, Bob Gross, the superintendent at the time, did not immediately say no to my crazy idea. I just about begged him to admit the girls, promising I would personally do whatever it took to make them eligible for enrollment. Bob was patient and open-minded but also realistic, more realistic than I was, I'm sure. He agreed to take the first step, which was to give both girls an assessment test. "Let's see how they do," he cautioned, "and decide after we see the results."

Since Cherry and Rathana would have to take the test in Singapore, it was time to talk to them. Rathana has a vivid memory of that moment:

> *That day when my mom first asked me about living in Singapore we were in the library reading "The Giving Tree." We read it over and over and over until I actually understood what the story was about. I just liked being with her even when I didn't understand a word she said! I tried to copy her and say the words as she did. And then she asked me, "Do you want to study, to have a better education?" And I said, "YES! Yes, that's what I want to do." And then she asked, "Would you like to come to Singapore?" I thought she was joking. Then Savy came and asked me, "Are you ready to live in Singapore?" and I knew. I didn't doubt myself and I didn't want to say no. My answer was, "YES, YES," off the top of my head. I didn't*

know what it meant back then. I just understood that I would get a better education.

Later that same day I asked Cherry if she would be interested in going to Singapore to study. She remembers being shocked:

I didn't really know what to do. I ran home and asked my parents, "Ma, what should I do? Dad, what should I do?" And they said, "You should do whatever you want. You decide." And I was like, "Okay, this is a really good opportunity to see a different world, a different culture, and learn new things, new experiences, so yeah, okay." But I knew it was BIG.

When I talked with Rathana's and Cherry's parents, Savy as usual served as my interpreter. He explained to them that the plan was to have the girls live with us for a year and see how it went. He tried to convey the many things they would be doing and learning and seeing. He described both SAS and our home. It helped that he had visited both. And he assured them that the girls would stay in regular contact with them, with frequent phone calls and visits during every school break.

Cherry's parents in particular, were enthusiastic. They understood she was being given an extraordinary opportunity, and Cherry was already a hard-working student, looked up to by the other kids. But I know the decision to let her go was not easy, particularly for Cherry's mother. Cherry is one of just two children and the only girl.

Rathana's family understood the opportunity at a more practical place, especially how it could lift her out of the poverty she had known her entire life and would likely always know. Just being assured of three meals a day would be something special.

As I left each home with the blessings of their parents I promised to care for the girls as if they were my own. It was an easy promise to make because I felt that degree of love for them.

Bill and I decided to ease into the situation by having the girls stay with us for a week in March of 2005 so they could take the assessment test and begin to get an idea of what living in the Amelio household would be like for them and for us. Then, if all went well, and assuming SAS admitted them, they would return a few months later before the start of the school year.

We welcomed Rathana and Cherry to our home with a little fanfare. We decorated the house with streamers and balloons and put up big welcome signs in the bedroom they would be sharing. Our boys were great and Bill was wonderful too, although we've since learned that his gruff playfulness made them nervous. Over the years Rathana and Cherry have come to appreciate his dry sense of humor, but back then it was a little scary for them.

We spent a quiet weekend together, but to the girls it was anything but uneventful. Just poking around the house, playing computer games with the other kids, listening to their music, and even flushing the toilets was an incredible adventure.

This was Rathana's second trip to Singapore, but Cherry had never left Cambodia before, so this first trip was particularly momentous for her. Our bathroom was a special mystery. She couldn't figure out how to work the toilet, and I had to show her how to take a bath for the first time.

She remembers the experience like this:

> I didn't really know what to do. I was like, "You just go in there and stay for what, for a long time?" I was really confused. And then my mom explained to me, "You just go in, lie there, and you just clean your body. For five minutes or ten minutes, you just lie there, and then after

that you rinse yourself. And then after that, you're clean."
So I said, "Okay! It's really, really weird, but I'll try it."

Not surprisingly, neither girl scored particularly well on the SAS assessment test, but Bob Gross was phenomenal and decided to give them a chance. It was both altruistic and courageous of him to take such a risk and we will always be grateful for his belief in the girls and in us.

By the time I took Rathana and Cherry back to Cambodia we were all excited about them coming back a few months later to live with us. We decided they would both enroll in the sixth grade. Cherry is a year younger than Rathana but they were at about the same level academically and I thought it was important that they be in the same class for a number of reasons. Not only could they support each other, but I would also be able to help them with the same homework. In addition, SAS wouldn't have to have two separate levels of assistance in the classroom.

Our biggest priority during these first few months was improving the girls' English skills. Fortunately, Bill Hannagan, the director of SAS' terrific English as a Second Language (ESL) program, was committed to finding the necessary teaching staff and other resources to help transition them into their new lives.

Their marvelous ESL teacher, Sharon Carroll, actually accompanied them through the hallway the first few weeks of school and for many years helped them maneuver through their studies. We hired her to tutor both girls and that made a big difference as well. Once they were able to communicate a little better, their confusion about almost everything began to lessen.

Everyone at SAS—the kids, the faculty, the administration, and the parents—were totally behind the girls' success. That's the only way it would have worked. The welcoming attitude started at the top, with Bill Hannagan personally telling the student body that these fabulous new Cambodian girls, who barely spoke a word of English, were matriculating through their school. He encouraged the other students to assist Rathana and Cherry in any way they could, and he assigned them buddies who stayed with them throughout the day. He thoughtfully chose classmates who had participated in at least one MAD trip to a CFC school because they knew a little something about where Rathana and Cherry had come from. The SAS administration also agreed to bend school policy to help them succeed. They allowed the girls to be graded pass/fail that first year, an unheard-of act of generosity that totally blew my mind.

Not surprisingly, Cherry and Rathana were in utter culture shock those first few months during the fall of 2005. Their English was next to nothing, and everything else was foreign to them as well. Much of our home time was spent learning words and helping them make sense of their countless new life experiences. English-Khmer dictionaries were always at hand, and every member of the Amelio family had his or her own copy.

Mostly the girls observed for themselves, everything from the chores they were expected to do around the house, to choosing what to eat in the cafeteria lunch line. They watched what the other kids did—where they put their books, how they used their lockers, how to get on a school bus and buckle their safety belts, and so much more. On top of that, they sat in classrooms, did their schoolwork, and of course dealt with the social intricacies of middle school. When I think back on those months I am in awe of both girls.

The Amelio household too spent the first few months trying to figure out how all this was going to work. Everything was a learning experience for all of us. Family outings like going to a restaurant, the beach, shopping, or out for ice cream became a chance to help Rathana and Cherry learn new things.

Riley, Bronson, Rathana, Cherry, and I loved watching silly cartoons together. The girls especially loved Bugs Bunny. At first they couldn't understand a word the characters were saying, but the physical humor said it all. They laughed and laughed, really deep belly laughs, something you seldom see Cambodian children do. They must have watched the movie *High School Musical* thirty times. They may not have understood what was being said, but they loved the singing and dancing and the obviously happy ending.

There were also some tough times early on. Cherry in particular was homesick, and as you can imagine, the hours spent in classrooms in which no one spoke their language were hugely challenging. Cherry explains:

> *The first week I came to Singapore, I pretty much missed my family. I didn't know much English and I didn't feel people understood me. I had no way of really sharing my feelings with other people. It was hard to be in class. I couldn't understand people talking, or the teacher explaining. I couldn't think straight. It was frustrating. I just didn't know how to speak English.*

Rathana's experience was similar:

> *All I knew in class was that a teacher was opening his mouth, and all I hear is MUTE. It would be traveling in the brain, like on a train traveling somewhere, but I don't know where it was going. I was thinking in Cambodian, the teacher was talking in English, and I didn't know what he was talking about. I didn't know what I was supposed to do. I just knew it was scary and I didn't understand ANYTHING.*
>
> *I was frustrated a lot when I couldn't do my home-work or when a teacher would say, "You don't have to turn it in until next week." I wanted to turn it in the same*

time as everyone else. I wanted to have grades. I wanted to be an actual student. I couldn't write. I couldn't read. I couldn't do my homework. It was just HARD.

Many times I doubted myself. I thought I was not smart enough, that I didn't understand my friends, and I missed my family. I'm Cambodian; I was so different from everybody else. They all looked smart and cool and knew what they were doing. Someone would say that the boy was "hot," and I would feel extremely stupid. "He is not on fire! Why would you say hot?" And they would go, "What are you talking about? He is on fire!" And I would say, "He is not on fire!" Why are you guys saying 'hot'?" I'd keep doubting myself because I didn't understand them.

Both girls, but particularly Rathana, also had some stomach issues due to the radical changes in their diet. If food has been scarce your entire life you will have a predictable response to suddenly eating three nutritious meals each day.

At the beginning when Rathana and Cherry sat down at the table, they would eat like there was no tomorrow. That first year we probably didn't say "No" enough. They adored spaghetti and asked for three or four helpings each time we ate it, something that would make any belly cry out.

Rathana also tended to get motion sickness in the car. The physical changes were just plain hard for her.

Bedtime was also difficult. That's when they missed their families the most. While we lived in Singapore, they visited their families in Siem Reap frequently, certainly every Christmas and spring and summer vacations, but those first weeks away from home were challenging for them.

One night not long after they had arrived I went into their room to check on them and they were both lying on the floor.

"Girls, come up to the bed," I told them.

They refused; they did not want to sleep in a bed. They said they had *never* slept in a bed and they wanted to sleep on the floor like they did in Cambodia. They also did not want to be covered by blankets because they had never slept with anything on top of them. They were not even accustomed to sheets. After all, in Cambodia they lived in one-room houses.

I lay down on the floor with them and we read a book together until they fell asleep. All the while I was thinking, *What have I gotten myself into?* I thought that a lot those first months, particularly when one of the girls was moody or difficult like any pre-teen, but then she would almost immediately do or say something that would just as quickly melt my heart.

There were so many gut-wrenching moments, like when I'd see them walk to the bus stop and board the bus, or when I observed how insepa-rable they were. They even showered together. I would cry as I asked myself, "Is this the right thing to have done? Who am I to say that my life is better and that this is better for them? Should I have taken them from their families?" I definitely questioned what I was doing, which I had never done before about anything related to CFC.

Negotiating school and friends gradually became easier once the girls began to have a better grasp of English. Meanwhile, Bill and I spent a lot of time encouraging them to express themselves as best they could.

An important time for us as a family has always been evening meals. Each night at the dinner table we have a tradition we call "highlights of the day" in which each person, including guests, is expected to recap their day's key moments.

For at least the first year we all kept our English-Khmer dictionaries beside us as Cherry and Rathana struggled to tell us what they had done that day. Cherry would sometimes prepare what she was going to say and memorize it in English. "But then I'd forget and have to open my dictionary anyway," she now giggles.

The girls did start to feel comfortable with the Amelio family pretty quickly, and that at least helped them feel grounded, to feel they had a safe place to return to each day after the bewilderment they experienced at school. We also really worked together as a family to get the girls to talk.

As Cherry says, "By the second year I was getting more comfortable and more confident in myself, especially once I could understand more English and could say what I wanted to say. And the family gave me a lot of love, and I just felt connected with them, like we were brother and sister."

Another decision that I think helped was my rule of "No Khmer spoken at home," though I knew this was hard for them. Whenever I heard them chattering in Khmer, I'd remind them, "English, girls; English only!"

I suppose it was the right thing to do. I believed we had to be tough about them learning English, a key to adjusting to their new lives. Every day they expressed themselves just a little better, and one day, almost like someone had pressed a button, they were speaking English. It really did seem like that, like a remote control was stuck on fast forward. Today the girls have even mastered teenage colloquial expressions, eye rolling and all.

I also pushed them to get involved in school activities. I thought that sports would be a universal language, but for diminutive Cherry, this presented just another challenge. I signed her up for every sport the school offered, including basketball, soccer, and softball. For a while gym class was a nightmare, but lo and behold, she ended up loving softball!

It sounds like tough love and I guess it was, but in the Amelio household tough love always comes with a warm hug. We do a lot of serious handholding that is quite foreign to Cambodians. If one of the girls did something wrong, or if I was trying to encourage them to try to do better,

I would hold their hands or hug them as I told them, "Look, no matter what, I love you." After a while I think they embraced (hah!) our hugging tradition with enthusiasm and understanding.

The girls also made a lot of friends that first year, including Alex McConaghy, Emily Martin, and Cassie Miller. That more than anything helped with their transition. When I put my ear to their door during sleepovers or school-related events and heard them all playing and giggling I couldn't stop myself from tearing up.

It also helped that both girls knew that plenty of people were rooting for them—not only their new family and community in Singapore, but also their family and friends in Cambodia. Cherry explains:

> My parent (in Cambodia) is the person who pushed me a lot. My mom didn't have much of an education because of the Khmer Rouge, so she wants me to believe in myself, and wants women to believe. I would NEVER give up because I want my family to be proud of me and so all the people in Cambodia could think that this little girl can do it, so I can do it.

Rathana always took a more worldly view. She was like that from the first time I met her in Spien Chrieve:

> I had a lot of help from my friends, from my mom, dad, teachers, and tutor. Everybody was willing to help. I think about the encouragement I got from people when I was down, how everybody was helping me. That's one of the things I told myself, that other people hadn't given up on me. That's something that kept me going.
>
> My mom's speech at ArtAid, talking about how she wanted to change the world and change Cambodia and how her present as a Mother's Day gift was a school,

made me realize that my coming to Singapore wasn't to be an "American girl." My goal was to come here to get an education, not to try and fit in with the girls at school. There was so much more for me to worry about than just trying to fit in. That's what made me realize that this is my dream, that I can't give up now.

A turning point for me occurred in January of 2006 when Rathana and Cherry returned to Singapore after visiting their families over the Christmas holiday. When I went to pick them up at the Singapore Airport all I could think was, "Here are my girls! They're coming home!" It felt so natural, like my own kids returning from summer camp. I just wanted Rathana and Cherry back and to return to the swing of things. Best of all, when they walked off the plane, I could see in their faces that they felt the same way.

The girls gradually became more and more familiar with us and with Western life, and our family with them. I think I know when I started thinking that all this might actually work out. It was in year two, when all the kids stopped being on their best behavior and started to argue like real brothers and sisters.

Remember, Rathana and Cherry were pre-teens when they came to live with us, and we all know the hormonal challenges posed by that age and the subsequent teenage years. We had the typical tears and displays of emotion, another characteristic contrary to the way Rathana and Cherry were raised. Cambodians don't cry. I had to explain to them that in my world it was okay to cry if they were frustrated, mad, sad, or even happy.

Watching the girls grow and adapt to their new environment has been one of the most remarkable experiences of my life, like watching a film strip of girls growing, coping, learning, blooming. Not all the changes have been completely positive, of course. What parent hasn't been exasperated with her teenager and what teenager hasn't decided at some point that her parents are dolts?

Adopted children also have challenges all their own, and Cherry and Rathana were dealing with two separate families. Nonetheless, I could see that they were adapting. In the early days, for instance, the girls were very careful and orderly about their space. They made their beds every day and put away their clothes in just the right place. They really respected and appreciated what they had. To take them shopping and get them a pair of shoes was an experience for all of us. But like many kids, they went through periods of entitlement in which they expected to be given rather than to earn the good things in life. This did not happen all the time by any means, but it happened, and it was something Bill and I worked hard to confront in all our kids.

Having Rathana and Cherry become part of our family changed us too. "We've had our share of struggles," says Bill. "We've had sibling rivalry that was difficult and we had to help the kids manage that, but I think that having them in our family has helped ground all our kids by learning the importance of sharing what you have."

Bill and I have also had a ringside seat watching them grow into young ladies. Bill says:

> It's been wonderful to watch them develop over the last six years—to see the successes and accomplishments they've had, but also the struggles and the way they've been able to rise above all the obstacles they faced and still have a solid connection with their families in Cambodia. That connection is still there with regular Skype calls. Yet here in America they're part of our family. They call Jamie and me "Mom" and "Dad." They're connected to all of our kids. It's been a privilege to watch, and the impact it has had on our family is quite amazing.

Rathana and Cherry also offered us a window into the changes we were making at our CFC schools, since they had experienced both the before and after. Rathana remembers it this way:

> *The first time I went to school in Cambodia I remember the grass being up to my waist and having to dig through it. My class had eighty-eight kids in it. Many of them would pay the teacher to pass them so they could go on to the next class, but some of us didn't have the money to pay the teacher, so no matter how hard we worked we would be at the bottom of the class.*
>
> *All we knew about going to school was sitting around the tables, listening to the teacher. It wasn't really about learning anything, but just being around people.*
>
> *People would never talk about their feelings, their problems, or what was going on at home. Or what they knew about the world or politics. We didn't think we had the right to talk about it. My parents, they told me not to talk about it because when they were growing up, during Pol Pot and the Khmer Rouge, they were not allowed to speak about their father or about politics or if they loved the king or what they learned at school. So I think that image of being afraid of your own people, of people around you, scares them. Sharing your feelings or wanting to change scares them. And they wanted to teach their children that way too. You're not supposed to share your feelings; you've got to hold them in because you don't want to die. So that's what the children did. They learned to hold it in and keep it out, always smiling. Smiling is the key.*

Sometimes the teachers didn't show up, or some-
times they had outside jobs or they had family business
to do. We would just sit in class until 5:00 o'clock or when
it was time to go home. We would start talking, laughing,
dancing. Or sometimes we would pretend we were teach-
ing, or we would make up a song about the rain.

But I couldn't really blame the teacher. She needed
the money to support her family. I was just frustrated
about the whole thing. It shouldn't work that way.

Cherry also remembers what school was like in Cambodia:

Our school didn't have much of a roof, so when it rained
we had to duck under the tables so we wouldn't get wet.
There were a lot of spider webs everywhere, and we didn't
really clean it. We didn't really care about the classroom
that much. Now when I go to Cambodia and see all the
change, it is really cool. We have art and drawings every-
where. And children sit reading library books. I was like,
"Oh my gosh, they actually learn things!" And they try
their best. It is really, really fun to see that.

Rathana agrees:

The teachers love teaching! They teach the children as
much as they can by getting them to talk, to communicate.
They're aware of the Cambodian environment and policy
and politics and they try to share that with the children.

Rathana (center left) and Cherry (center right) at the Kong Much opening ceremony.
Christy and Madi Miller are to the right of Cherry; Jill Kirwin is to the left of Rathana.
and Bronson is behind her.

Predicting your children's future is a fool's errand, but if I were to guess, I would say that Cherry will probably be the one to return to Cambodia. She's always saying that whatever she does, she wants to give back to her country.

Rathana is more the artistic type. I can imagine her going to school in Paris someday. But then again, Rathana says she wants to return to live in Cambodia too, so maybe after Paris?

Rathana says:

> *After living with the Amelio family, I questioned the world. I questioned a lot: "What's my purpose here? What am I doing here? What am I going to do with my education? What am I going to do in Cambodia?"*
>
> *I do believe that everybody is here for a purpose. One is to help others, and the other is to help yourself. By helping others, without realizing it you are helping*

yourself too. And with this education I am having, I definitely want to go back and share my story with the children of Cambodia. I will tell them that everybody has a purpose and that my purpose is to come back and share my words with my people, telling them not to be afraid, not to be afraid of change.

My mom in Cambodia would always tell me that wherever you are in life, you have to go as the river flows. You have to turn, you have to twist, you have to go backwards if that's where it's taking you. Like a river, life is always up and bouncing, bumpy, smooth, turning left or right. But if you want to go toward your destiny, toward your dreams and hopes, you have to turn the way it takes you. If it tells you to go right, you have go to the right. If it's bumpy, you have go with the bumps, and if it's smooth, sometimes it's just like that. Life is smooth and bumpy and you have to go with it.

I constantly tell Rathana and Cherry that if any two kids can do something amazing with their lives, they can. They already have.

"You came to a country where everyone spoke English but you spoke none," I remind them. "You never should have made it at SAS, but you did. Not only that, but by the time you left, you were on the honor role."

They are my heroes.

EIGHT

Turning Orange to Gold

As the 2006–'07 school year began, we were laser-focused on continuing to improve the three CFC schools we had already adopted. In order to do that, we needed to strengthen CFC's infrastructure in Singapore.

Improvement from an organizational perspective meant many things, but first and foremost it meant enhancing our ability to raise money, and we began to take proactive steps to expand our base of support in Singapore as well as elsewhere, particularly the United States.

To even begin a fundraising effort in America we would have to become a 501(c)(3) not-for-profit organization, a daunting task for someone like me who tends to blanch at bureaucratic regulations, forms, and legalese. As was so frequently the case with CFC, we found help from an unexpected source, in this case our ten-year-old son Riley.

Riley's teachers were always interested in our efforts. One of them, Kate Bucknall, along with her husband Ron Starker, became very involved and participated in several teacher training trips. Then Riley delivered a second grade show-and-tell presentation about his parents that included my work in Cambodia. A regular visitor to Siem Reap, Riley must have painted a vivid picture of the schools and village because his presentation provoked a lengthy class discussion. Later he told me his friend Sophie couldn't stop talking about it.

A few days later I ran into Sophie's mom, Mae Anderson, who asked what she could do to help. I told her about our need to establish CFC as a 501(c)(3) and how I had been procrastinating, mainly because I was at a loss as to where to begin. Suddenly she was telling me that her husband Joe worked at the international law firm Morrison & Foerster in downtown Singapore. Next thing I knew she had volunteered him to set up Caring for Cambodia as a non-profit organization registered in the United States.

That's just how it went with CFC. As soon as I identified a need I would stumble on an expert who turned orange and helped me fill it. It happened like this a hundred times. One of my kids would talk to one of their friends and it would get back to their parents, a Tanglin Trust or SAS teacher would become inspired, or a tourist would be agog at what was happening at one of our schools, and pretty soon we'd have another member to add to our increasing swell of volunteers.

The support we've received from the two largest international schools in Singapore, SAS and Tanglin Trust, has been particularly crucial. In addition to countless teacher training trips, students and teachers from both schools have volunteered to create teaching materials, host fundraisers (everything from bake sales to dinner dances), and collect toothbrushes, backpacks, and first aid and hygiene kits. They've also participated in various projects in Siem Reap, either in conjunction with scheduled teacher training sessions or during separate visits.

The Tanglin Trust School, for example, almost singlehandedly created a teachers resource center at one of our newest schools in the village of Aranh. SAS sponsors a high school club that has developed a number of interactive programs in Spien Chrieve, everything from Bingo events (a great way to learn English numbers) to volleyball. The club members also have had great fun painting tables at our school in Kong Much.

To replicate these successes, CFC has recently launched sister school programs all over the world with educational institutions that commit to supporting CFC. Support can mean funding, but also activities like pen-pal programs and collection campaigns for designated school supplies.

The development of our website is another story of how people appear on our doorstep to help. The international advertising and public relations firm Ogilvy & Mather was doing some work for Dell when Bill was in charge of Dell's Asia Pacific region. Ogilvy's chairman, Shelly Lazarus, happened to mention that Ogilvy was planning a team-building meeting in Siem Reap. After Bill talked to Shelly about CFC, Ogilvy expanded its trip to include installing a playground at Kong Much and building a small hut to serve as a cultural center now run by Loeum, one of our Cambodian mentor teachers.

The best thing that came out of that visit was our introduction to Chris Graves, now the global CEO of Ogilvy Public Relations Worldwide and an invaluable CFC board member. By his own admission, that team-building trip turned Chris orange. The photos he took, mostly of huge, joyous smiles on the faces of the children, are still on his phone. One photo in particular sticks with him, of a tiny student sitting on the shoulders of a large, brawny Ogilvy executive, using him as a ladder while painting high up where the wall meets the ceiling.

The Ogilvy group painted every square inch of the school and built a brand new playground too. As was usually the case, everyone sang as they worked, mostly off-key and punctuated by laughter, with multiple kids scurrying about, caught up in the excitement and wanting to help.

Chris tells the rest of his story in his own words:

> As we always do, Ogilvy looks for opportunities to do service work in every community where we hold a significant, company-wide meeting. In this case, Caring for Cambodia was something we felt really hit the mark in terms of our modest help having an out-sized impact.
>
> In addition to painting the school, we also delivered more than one hundred shiny brand new red bicycles. We came to understand that while a bike is a magical thing for any child, in this case it meant family transportation, a crucial factor in engaging with the community and ensuring the child makes it to school. Then the most amazing thing happened. We brought out buckets of different colored paint so they could paint the bikes any way they wanted. It was a riotous, giggling, multicolored circus as the kids made the bikes their own.
>
> I knew at the end of that day that I could do more, and whatever tiny bit I did would have a huge impact. So often when we are asked to help charities, causes, or foundations, we do so out of duty or just to go along with the crowd, but frankly, we don't feel we make much of a difference.
>
> That's not the case with Caring for Cambodia. In a tiny country where the United States dropped more bombs than fell during all of World War II, in a nation in which a third of the population was massacred by its

own despots, where teachers were executed and all hope had been exterminated, Caring for Cambodia asked a big "What if?" question: what if we could rekindle the light of Cambodia's children one great school at a time? I was thrilled when Jamie and Bill asked Ogilvy to help.

After Chris' visit, a young, digitally-savvy team of Ogilvy volunteers led by Charlie Tansill created a beautiful, fully functional website to tell the story of Caring for Cambodia.

We've had the support of many great people over the years, and once they turn orange they tend to stay that way. I'm always in awe of the emotional commitment people make, and it still astonishes me to think that the meetings that began with a few women in my living room have morphed into hundreds of people from around the world sharing email messages, or a dozen professsionals sitting in a boardroom, or me at a lectern giving a speech, often accompanied by a PowerPoint or a video presentation.

Although I've told the same story a hundred times, the tears still come. Something always happens to me when I think of the moment I met Srelin for the first time, and of how much CFC has accomplished and how many lives we've been able to change.

Equally powerful is the feeling that CFC has changed *us*. I've seen people in these meetings transform before my eyes as they realize what a powerful difference they can make and how incredibly blessed and privileged we all are. I leave every meeting on cloud nine. I absolutely love what I do, and I am determined to inspire more people to become involved. I want everyone to know there is a job for them in CFC. Their special talent is needed somewhere, somehow.

I also have many wonderful memories of bonding with other CFC volunteers at meetings, at fundraisers, and on MAD trips. The memory of riding bicycles with Darla Bryans, Eve Denoma, and Dee Gallo and humming the marching tune from the *Wizard of Oz*, laughing together that we aren't in Kansas any more, always brings a smile to my face, and I'm not the only one who has these feelings.

One year Lisa Wiesel, a parent from SAS, volunteered to work at ArtAid, one of our annual fundraising events. I bumped into her a few months later, and before we could even say hello she started crying. I hugged her with tears in my eyes too and said, "Now you know."

"Yes I do," she said. We did not have to say anything else. This kind of thing happens all the time. I often wonder if volunteers like Christy Machulsky and Renee Chipman know how grateful I am. Do they and the hundreds of other volunteers know that as I go about my day, take a jog, drive my kids to soccer practice, or cook dinner, I wipe away tears when I think of all they do?

Does it matter what I think? I hope they feel the good. Surely they know that what they do makes the world a better place. It's funny how strongly I believe that we are changing history by changing children's lives, their schools, and an entire country. I believe this with every bit of who I am, even when CFC encounters growing pains.

Inevitably, working with dozens of women volunteers, mingling with all different types of personalities, results in drama from time to time. Volunteers do not always get along and talk behind each other's backs.

At one point the bad energy was getting out of hand, with tears and apologies at every event, so much so that I began to feel like a school guidance counselor. In addition to the challenge of CFC, I was being asked to offer feedback on how my friends should behave and grow. It was just too much. Not that I was blameless, mind you. I can be abrupt and impatient at times. I know I sometimes hurt people's feelings along the way. One of my regular mantras is "Ten lines," which is my way of telling people to get to the point and do what they say they are going to do.

To cope with this challenge, I started reading about volunteerism and constantly asking Bill for advice. I also prayed for guidance. I wanted to be a good role model, someone who was doing the right thing in all areas of my life. Clearly I wasn't doing such a great job of controlling my teenager, but I could control how I portrayed myself and the effort I put in to being grounded.

Virginia was a huge help to me in this regard. Talking to her almost every day gave me perspective, and occasionally I took a deep breath and stepped back for a moment. Once for an entire week I attempted to talk only with Virginia and my family and not to my friends in Singapore who were fighting among themselves.

I think the daily job of volunteer management should be taught in business schools. How do you get people to want to do something just because it's the right thing to do? How do you get people to do what they say they are going to do, even though there is no paycheck?

Over the years my intuition about people has become pretty good. I now find myself associating certain colors and feelings with those volunteers I know will stay the course. I look for bright colors, like orange of course, but I also see also pinks, purple, and a very light blue. When I see beige, it means the volunteer won't follow through, and red means they want to, but probably won't always be successful. Kooky, huh?

I've also learned that there are several types of volunteers. First, there are those who show up at meetings because they are your friends, but they don't turn orange. Eventually their commitment tends to wane.

There are those who talk and talk about the million tasks they are going to take on but who get nothing done.

There are those who want to help because it's the right thing to do but fail to follow through. When they see you, they come right out and tell you why they couldn't get the job done. Often these people can be inspired to do more.

There are those who year after year squeeze CFC into their busy lives. Their intentions are good, but they may only have time to participate in one event a year or take on something behind the scenes. They make an important contribution to CFC and for the most part stay orange.

Finally, there are those who lead busy lives but who make an ongoing commitment to CFC. They are selfless and incredibly hard-working, and they do what they say they are going to do, no matter what.

The common denominator among virtually everyone who gives their time or writes a check to CFC is that they are orange. In short, they make CFC possible.

Robin Hood and Adrian Hobbs

Unfortunately, there are always a few bad seeds. Although these individuals are the exception, they can be dangerous. As careful as we tried to be, we found ourselves taken advantage of on at least two memorable occasions. The first time involved a man named Robin Hood who contacted Bill, offering to take six months off from work and move to Siem Reap as a volunteer. (Yes, that was really his name—Robin Hood.) This must have been 2004 or 2005 because Bill was still at Dell. Robin drove to Cambodia from his home in Penang, Malaysia, promising to teach English at our schools and to film a documentary about CFC.

For a while everything seemed great. I even bought Robin a video camera to use. But after a month or so he suddenly started sending me strange emails suggesting how we should change things, listing which NGOs we should partner with, and inviting all sorts of people to our schools. I was constantly having to pull him back.

My discomfort grew when Savy, who doesn't have a bad word to say against anyone, began hinting that things were not so great with Robin and that the teachers didn't like him. Finally Savy wrote me a long note telling me that in front of a classroom of kids Robin Hood had yelled at the teacher. He added that the children were so scared of him that they wouldn't come back to class.

Bill helped me write a note firing him, and when Robin left Siem Reap he started blogging horrible stuff about CFC, saying that Savy was taking money and that I was blind to what was really going on. We had been supporting his efforts, even paying for his film, and now the documentary he was supposedly working on had turned completely negative and he was trying to poison CFC's reputation.

"I'm going to tell the real story," he warned us. None of his charges had any basis in fact, but the idea that someone was out there posting terrible things about us on the Internet really disturbed me.

Michael O'Neill, another angel who joined our board after his first trip to Siem Reap, is our volunteer legal counsel. He finally scared Robin off, but it took years for Robin's libelous blogs to completely disappear from the web.

A much bigger disaster occurred a few years later in connection with a Diana Krall concert. In early 2008 I received an email from a man named Adrian Hobbs telling me he was looking for an organization to sponsor a concert by one of his clients, Diana Krall, as a fundraising event.

Hobbs owned a few restaurants in Singapore, had read about CFC, and wanted to give back and help in some way. He told me that his entertainment company also managed Mariah Carey and the Catalan tenor, Jose Carreras.

I met with Hobbs and liked his idea. A new marina was about to open at the harbor on Keppel Bay and he proposed to inaugurate it with a Diana Krall concert. We could offer different levels of tickets, including a VIP package, and a portion of the proceeds would go to CFC.

In retrospect, I should have done a better job of due diligence, but I was in frequent contact with people who worked for Hobbs and he seemed like a legitimate businessman. Bill and I had dinner with him at one of his restaurants and I felt great sympathy for him when he told us a horribly sad story about how his baby had died the year before after a long vigil at the hospital. Something about him didn't sit right with Bill, but I said, "Come on, give the guy a chance." I even met his wife and new baby, and Hobbs definitely seemed to know what he was talking about. He promised to do a lot of promotion and to make the concert a real happening by combining it with Singapore's first Formula One race through the city. He also hinted that at some point he might be able to get Diana Krall to visit Siem Reap, explaining that a few years earlier he had been responsible for a sold-out Jose Carreras concert at Angkor Wat that had created a huge buzz. It turned out Raffles had been the sponsor, which seemed perfect, since CFC had a great relationship with the hotel. With such connections, what could possibly go wrong?

I sent a mass email to all our supporters in Singapore telling them we were selling $1,500 VIP tickets to see Diana Krall that would include a pre-show cocktail party, a back stage pass, seats in the first ten rows, refreshments throughout the show, and a post-concert party on board the super yacht, *The Ulin Utame*. Simultaneously, I spoke to Joe Anderson at Morrison & Foerster about the different permits we would need. Given Singapore's strict fundraising guidelines, we decided it would be best to run everything through Hobbs' organization and have CFC be the recipient of a portion of the proceeds. I met with Hobbs regularly and he seemed to have everything under control, so Bill and I agreed to advance the up-front costs.

Our first payment to Hobbs was a little more than we had expected, but he told us we really had to get this going because otherwise someone else would grab the venue. CFC was going to make as much as $300,000 on the event, or so we thought, so Bill and I wrote him a personal check.

This was the first week of June 2008, just as we were returning to Austin for the summer. Hobbs and I agreed we would talk every other week and that he would give me regular updates, but gradually it became more and more difficult to reach him by email or phone. He was either out of town, or I had just missed him, or he had changed his telephone number. I was starting to get nervous.

Meanwhile, we made a second payment to his company and tickets for the concert were going fast. About twenty people bought the VIP package and many more purchased less expensive tickets.

By the time we returned to Singapore in August Hobbs had completely disappeared. His restaurants had mysteriously closed and no one answered his office phone. It was now just a few weeks before the September event.

Because Bill and I felt personally responsible for the disaster, we decided to pay back everyone out of our own pocket. Diana Krall did perform, but at a different venue in Fort Canning Park, and the concert was a mess. People sat in rickety white plastic chairs and the music could barely be heard over the noise of the runners congregating nearby.

In the days after the event I considered trying to contact Diana Krall, but I was drained and I decided to put it behind me. My energy was better spent on CFC. Besides, I had no reason to believe she knew anything about the scam, so what could I expect her to do?

We subsequently learned that Hobbs did own an entertainment company, but he was not Diana Krall's manager. He had made it seem like he talked to her every day, but that wasn't even close to the truth. Liz King's husband filed an official police report on Hobbs that allowed the embassy to flag him as someone not to do business with. I think I would have sued him if we could have found him.

We kept all this quiet for a long time, but finally it came out that Bill and I were on the hook personally. We took a tremendous hit. I had to do a lot of self-talk to get over this one. As usual, Bill was incredibly supportive, but the experience was devastating.

Creative Fundraising

I coped by throwing myself into CFC. By this time, thanks to Joe Anderson's efforts, we were designated by the IRS as a 501(c)(3) not-for-profit organization in the U.S and we had an Internet presence thanks to Chris Graves, Charlie Tansill, and Ogilvy.

To my surprise, I learned pretty quickly that these two assets did not translate into immediate fundraising success. We found it difficult to coordinate fundraising in the United States since we had no real foothold there, and most of our funds continued to come from supporters in Singapore. Only after Bill and I moved back to Texas in 2010 were we able to build a support base in the United States, an effort that continues to be a major priority today.

We did, however, shake things up in Singapore. Our fundraising committee was constantly organizing new events, many of which became annual CFC traditions. Creativity is the backbone of many on our team, as evidenced by dance-a-thons, Bunko nights, private concerts, and making gorgeous jewelry. Tammy Hong, a great friend and solid CFC supporter, used her creativity to design and sell stunning CFC greeting cards with Brazilian artist Heloiza Montuori. Tammy was also instrumental in contributing to several other events that enabled us to aim higher and build more schools. I can never sufficiently thank these volunteers, but it is the most wonderful thing in the world to see.

Probably our biggest bi-annual fundraiser is our ArtAid charity event at which we auction off the works of established and emerging artists, as well as our own CFC students. Many people are responsible for its success, including Donna Coughlin, who became the event's first chairperson, and Heloiza, who regularly donates her paintings to our auctions and held special exhibitions at her house when she lived in Singapore. For the most recent ArtAid, Heloiza made the trip all the way from Brazil to help out and work with the kids.

Another ArtAid chairperson, Sandra Smith, works as if CFC is her full-time job. She solves every problem as soon as it appears, while simultaneously juggling the raising of three children with her husband Brent, a CFC board member. And Chris Churcher and his wife Charlie have more than once allowed us to hold the event at their Red Sea Gallery on Dempsey Road in Singapore.

ArtAid works out great because not only does it raise funds to support CFC, but we've also used it to create specific programs at our schools. For the past several years professional photographers and artists have visited our campuses in Siem Reap in order to share their work and mentor some of our students. When Martha Chaudry gave each student a digital camera that allowed them to photograph their world for the first time, the results were truly stunning.

Our CFC Caring Teas have also captured the interest and imagination of women in Singapore. Great food and exotic teas are served, but they have also evolved into exclusive afternoon events. In the early years they were held at people's homes; now we use one of Singapore's boutique hotels. The teas feature uniquely designed tabletops complete with dishes, glassware, cutlery, linens, centerpieces, and anything else these creative women can dream up. Place settings are laid out as unique pieces of art and guests walk around and look at them like they would in a museum, after which they have the opportunity to win a set in a raffle. The Mad Hatter and Alice should be so lucky as to have high tea in such elegant surroundings.

The teas are great fun, and have also become fundraising "happenings" that allow volunteers, amateur designers, business owners, or just a friend from next door to put their personal signatures on some incredible table settings. We've had Valentine's Day tables, Thanksgiving tables, men's gaming tables, little girls' birthday party tables, and one year, a particularly memorable Christmas table created by longtime supporter Michelle Smith.

We've created a template called "Easy As 1-2-3 Steps to Hosting a Caring Tea" so that anyone, anywhere, can organize a similar event. The final words of the manual read, "Make it your own. Make it unique. Make it Tea-riffic!" The slogan might be a little corny, but it works.

A lot of the credit for the success of the teas goes to Kelly Zotos, who has chaired the event almost every year since its inception. She is another woman who has an incredibly supportive husband, a common thread among the powerhouses of CFC.

We have also had plenty of corporate support over the years, as many companies have made Caring for Cambodia part of their commitment to their corporate social responsibility programs. Along with financial help, they have donated computers, bicycles, toothbrushes, uniforms, school supplies, and books; have become involved in our MAD or corporate team-building trips building homes and schools; have given us technical support and legal advice; and have hosted serious fundraisers.

Clean Water

We are always looking for ways to focus our volunteer campaigns on activities that will have an affirmative impact on the children in our Siem Reap schools. As a byproduct, we have found that much of our corporate giving extends beyond our campuses and into the surrounding communities.

For example, the toothbrushes and health and hygiene packages we distribute at each of our schools regularly make their way into the community. I've been to many homes in which I've seen a toothbrush or bar of soap that I'm sure came from CFC. I've also seen children's artwork on the wall, which I think is a direct result of the child's participation in ArtAid.

Probably our most important in-kind gift has been the water filtration systems installed at every CFC school by Mark Steele's Asia Water Foundation (AWF). One of Cambodia's biggest problems is its lack of healthy drinking water, coupled with a population that does not understand the importance of clean water for drinking and bathing. Those of us in the West take this precious natural resource for granted, but CFC children still routinely express their delight when water comes out of a drinking fountain simply by pressing a button, or when by opening a spigot, clear, drinkable water magically spurts out.

A priority of our health and hygiene initiative is teaching and reinforcing the importance of drinking clean water and the simple but necessary act of frequent hand washing, particularly before eating. We also know from experience that this message can only be driven home if it is reinforced in the home. Nothing is going to change until adults understand that washing and defecating in the same river bank they drink from causes disease, and that dysentery can be deadly if not properly treated. We decided early on that any grade school curriculum would have to emphasize hygiene and nutrition at least as much as it did reading, writing, and arithmetic.

The obvious first step for us in this regard was making certain our kids had access to clean drinking water when they came to school. When I learned that the price of a new well was only $150, we had new wells dug at each of our schools. While this water was safer than what our students had access to at home, it still contained dangerously high levels of pathogenic microorganisms. Then Mark Steele came along and changed everything.

Remarkably, AWF's system treats water without chemicals. A manual (not a gift of burden) pump sends the water up to a holding tank, where a filter purifies and stores the water. During the filtration process, bacteria, viruses, pathogens, and other contaminates are removed. Gravity then sends the clean water down through pipes, making it available for drinking and hand washing.

Clean hands and teeth thanks to Mark Steele and the Asia Water Foundation.

These filtrated water systems are used every day by every CFC student and have also become places for the community to gather. As villagers become aware of the connection between safe water and health, they can increasingly be seen hauling water from one of our schools back home for their cooking and other personal needs.

Bringing Siem Reap to Singapore

As part of our determination to connect our volunteer and fundraising activities in Singapore with our efforts on the ground in Cambodia, we have always encouraged our volunteers to visit Siem Reap to see for themselves the impact CFC is having on the schools and the surrounding communities.

By 2007 we were regularly sending teachers from Singapore (mostly from SAS and Tanglin Trust) to Siem Reap to conduct teacher training. This was clearly having an impact on the way teachers were teaching and students were learning, but I wanted this to be a two-way street. I decided it would also be a good idea to bring Savy and a group of accomplished CFC-trained administrators and teachers to Singapore to observe for themselves the teaching methods in place at SAS and Tanglin Trust.

Initially, not everyone supported the idea. I got a lot of pushback that it wasn't right to bring teachers from a poor village in Cambodia to observe super wealthy schools because it would be alarming, and even disheartening. But I dug my heels in pretty deep. I understood the apprehension, but in my gut I was convinced that seeing how children learned and teachers taught in the modern world would be inspiring and would help catapult our CFC teachers to the next level.

Sure enough, the first visit, funded by a grant from the Temasek Foundation and the National Institute of Education (NIE) in Singapore, was a life-changing experience for the dozen or so teachers and principals who participated. Often the smallest of moments made the biggest impression, such as learning how to use a shower, or inserting a plastic card to open a hotel room door. Elevators proved to be enormously popular, with grown men and women standing inside pushing buttons and giggling as the numbers lit up and they were magically carried up and down to the floor of their choice.

The most exciting part of the trip occurred at the SAS and Tanglin Trust schools, as the Cambodian teachers and administrators sat in classrooms, eyes opened wide. It didn't matter that they couldn't understand English. They saw how their Singapore counterparts directed the flow of classroom learning and how resources could be used in ways they had never imagined. Most of them feverishly took notes to keep track of the enormous amount of information they were trying to process.

They were especially elated when, walking through the hallways at SAS or Tanglin Trust, they ran into a teacher trainer who had worked with them in Siem Reap. Somehow that made a special connection between what the teacher trainers had been telling them and what they saw in practice in Singapore, and it created a special bond between the two worlds.

As important as any other experience was sitting down in one of our homes for tea and cookies or having a beer together. All told, this visit to Singapore created a deeper understanding that at the most profound place, we were all the same. We all loved our children and wanted the best for them.

To document their visit, we gave each teacher a disposable camera and everyone went home with a photo album bursting with visual memories to show their students. Before they left we also took the opportunity to introduce the Cambodian teachers to new methods and resources, thinking that if they saw a teaching resource they thought they could use in Siem Reap, CFC would make it available to them.

Turns out the reality was even better than that. Rather than just handing them the resources that worked well in Singapore, our CFC teachers wound up adapting them to their own needs.

For example, the Cambodian teachers were totally enamored by the large bulletin boards each SAS and Tanglin Trust classroom used to post everything from homework assignments, to signup sheets, to artwork. Immediately Kaye Bach and I started discussing where we might purchase enough bulletin boards for every CFC classroom and how to get them through customs. But Savy chimed in, "No, no, no. We can build them in Cambodia!"

The boards we used in Singapore were made of cork. This was unavailable in Cambodia, but Savy came up with an ingenious solution. A group of villagers who lived near the Amelio School were already weaving local vegetation into floor mats to sell to tourists. We hired them to put the matting into frames built by local carpenters, and presto! We had Cambodian-style bulletin boards.

The best thing about this is not that bulletin boards can today be found in every CFC classroom or that they have become so popular that dozens of non-CFC schools also use them. The icing on the cake is that our needs became a catalyst for a successful local business.

This is the kind of success we are trying to replicate. To that end, we made the tactical decision to abandon our policy of bringing resources like laminated posters or oversized books to Siem Reap from Singapore, even while we simultaneously continued to work closely with Cambodia's Ministry of Education to encourage non-CFC schools to use both our teaching methods and teaching tools. We knew this would only work if the teaching materials we suggested could be created in Cambodia at a reasonable cost, so that too became an important part of our outreach efforts.

Visits by Cambodian teachers to Singapore are now an annual event, one that continues to grow and evolve. Our largest trip took place in 2009, when thirty-five CFC teachers and administrators were chosen to take part in a two-week training seminar, again in collaboration with the Temasek Foundation and Singapore's NIE. Most days they spent six hours attending teacher training classes at the NIE. They were wowed by the teaching tips, but also by the modern English language tutorial rooms, computer labs, and large gymnasium. Their delight was so great, it was as if they were taking their first trip to Disneyland—or perhaps Epcot.

The group of administrators, which included three representatives from Cambodia's Ministry of Education, were just as inspired and passionate as the teachers. Savy reported that their discussions during morning and afternoon tea breaks and over dinner centered around what they were learning. This thrilled us because these were the people who had the authority to implement these teaching methods into Siem Reap's entire educational system.

The growing friendships and professional relationships developing between teachers from Singapore and Cambodia aside, the greatest achievement of these visits is what happens when the teachers and administrators return home. These individuals have successfully reached a certain level of accomplishment, and upon their return they commit to sharing what they have learned with their colleagues. We encourage this by organizing workshops where they talk to both CFC and non-CFC teachers. Many of the participants have also become mentor teachers. It is a real "pay it forward" experience.

Full-Time Teacher Trainer Changes Everything

While we believed we were making giant strides with our teacher training, both Kaye Bach and Katie Samson, our main coordinators in Singapore, were becoming frustrated. Relying on short, three-day workshops to teach goals and methods and hoping they would stick was not ideal. The lessons were not repeated or reinforced until the CFC teachers returned a few months later, which meant Kaye's "three times" rule was taking way too long to implement.

At lunch together in Singapore one day Kaye confessed to Katie, "You know, if there was ever a need for someone to come and stay in Siem Reap, I'd be the first to put up my hand."

That brief sentence changed the course of CFC. Katie repeated this conversation to Liz King and me, and we both had the same idea: to get the process started that would see Kaye working in Siem Reap full time.

Kaye was a bit startled at how her off-the-cuff comment produced such immediate results, but not surprisingly, she stuck by her words.

"The one thing I knew from my visits to the schools was what a big job this was going to be, not something that could be achieved by working part time," she remembers. "The teachers were going to need a total change in mindset. But I also sensed that many of them were eager for that change."

Fortunately for us, Kaye's husband George has always been an overwhelming supporter of her involvement with CFC. Singapore was only a two-hour flight away, but Kaye's departure would mean that after decades together the Bachs would now have a long-distance marriage. As far as I'm concerned that makes George one of the unsung heroes of CFC.

In August of 2008 Kaye took a leave of absence from SAS. With George's blessing, she moved to Siem Reap. Originally the plan was for her to stay a year but she ended up staying two.

For the first few months Kaye lived outside Spien Chrieve in what she called a tree house. Owned by a group of New Zealanders, it was actually just a typical Cambodian house on stilts. After she awoke one evening in the middle of the night to find a burglar in her bedroom and the guard posted outside sound asleep, she moved into downtown Siem Reap and was much more comfortable there.

Kaye was the expert in early childhood education, not me, so the only advice I gave her was a recap of the most important lesson I had learned over the course of the previous five years.

"It's all about building relationships," I told her. "The people and local communities have to trust us. They have to believe we are committed to the schools for the long term and that we will do exactly what we say."

Just the fact that Kaye was moving to Siem Reap as a full time CFC teacher trainer was going to send a powerful statement to this effect.

Kaye spent her first three weeks in intensive discussions with Savy. The Cambodian schools were on holiday, so for a few hours each day he briefed her about the schools, their greatest needs, and how they could best address them.

Kaye recalls thinking, "I didn't want to be perceived as a foreigner coming in with all the answers. I did not have most of the answers. Instead, my attitude was, 'Hey, what do you need and how can we best support you?'"

Together, Kaye and Savy articulated our goals into four overarching objectives:

- To improve the professionalism of CFC teachers, starting with getting them to come to school on time every day and *wanting* to come to school each day.
- To improve the school environment and make it more engaging for students.
- To increase the student population by increasing enrollment and by decreasing the dropout rate, even if it meant teachers going door-to-door to round up students.
- To educate parents in the villages so they recognized the value of sending their children to school.

Out of her discussions with Savy Kaye then crafted a three-week teacher-training workshop that would take place in September, prior to the start of the new school year, targeted at both teachers and administrators.

Once again Kaye decided it would be best to start with the lower grades and work her way up, so she began with the kindergarten and first grade teachers. The curriculum was grounded in the requirements of Cambodia's Ministry of Education and UNESCO's Child Friendly School program, but it also reflected the specific lessons CFC had developed during the previous few years.

Week one of the workshop was geared to kindergarten and first and second grade teachers; week two was for teachers in grades three and four; and week three was for teachers in grades five and six. CFC staff and education ministry representatives were also invited. One representative, Chang Rom, attended all three sessions. He was excited about what we were doing and wanted to be a part of it, telling us that we were giving him and others the power to help make changes in Cambodia's entire public school system. This was very exciting to hear, as it precisely mirrored our long-term goal.

In addition to teachers from our schools in Spien Chrieve, Bakong, and Kong Much, we also invited teachers from the village of Aranh to Kaye's first three-week training session. We had our eye on Aranh as our next school to adopt, but we were still a little wary of taking it on. Its physical condition was a mess, although perhaps no worse than the schools in Bakong or Kong Much had been. At this point we were watching to see how the teachers in Aranh responded to our training. Two women in particular, both of whom taught the older grades, were especially motivated and curious. Kaye promised them that if all went well their day would come to be part of CFC.

The training sessions focused on grade-appropriate projects and games that Kaye and Savy developed and that Kaye wanted the teachers to replicate in their classrooms. They also focused on what it meant to be a professional. Kaye and Savy discussed how it was the teachers' responsibility to beautify their classrooms and campuses, turning them into places where students *and* teachers wanted to spend time, and that it was their responsibility to pass that pride on to their students.

It was an old message, but one that consistently needed reinforcing. The difference now was that Kaye would be present as a full-time resource to help teachers follow up and implement these ideas.

Star Teachers and Star Students

Kaye quickly settled into a routine. Each morning Savy would pick her up in the CFC van and the two of them would have their daily meeting about that day's activities, as well as strategy sessions about CFC's long-range goals. When Kaye wasn't conducting a teacher training session they would visit one of our schools, observing and taking notes on the many improvements that needed to be made.

All of this was communicated by Savy, who acted as translator. When having only one translator became problematic, we hired Has Piseth full time. This freed up Savy's time enormously and allowed him to focus on other pressing matters.

Yet even after we hired Has Piseth Kaye continued to feel that the language barrier was slowing down the learning process between her and the teachers. It became apparent that she would need more than translators to communicate the ideas she was trying to convey to the teachers, almost all of whom spoke no English.

Meanwhile, some real stars were emerging among the teachers we were training. A handful of extremely creative, competent instructors were displaying skills not only at the training sessions, but also in their own classrooms, and Kaye chose two of them to become "mentor teachers."

In return for a small stipend, Chan Vandy, at this point a kindergarten teacher at the Amelio School, and Chea Sophea, a first grade teacher

also at the Amelio School, began to serve double-duty as mentors in the morning and classroom teachers in the afternoon. Each morning they met with Kaye to discuss the curriculum and programming for the upcoming week, which they subsequently presented at weekly lunch meetings for all kindergarten and first grade CFC teachers.

These mentor teachers also accompanied Kaye on unscheduled visits to observe how well the teachers were implementing their lesson plans. At first they told the teachers in advance when they were going to visit, but they soon discovered that some would put on a great show if they knew Kaye and the mentors were about to arrive. The solution was simple: Kaye and the mentor teachers began arriving unannounced.

Being a mentor has now become a personal goal for many of our teachers, and it led to a parallel initiative Kaye developed called "Star of the Week" that recognizes outstanding K–5 students. All elementary school children have the chance to be chosen as "Star of the Week," to wear a special crown, and to have their name posted on the wall. The children also take a notice home that gives their parents a chance to participate in the positive reinforcement. The opportunity to be acknowledged for excellence has proven to be a huge incentive for both students and teachers.

Education Starts Early

Meanwhile, one of our biggest challenges continued to be getting the parents of our students to understand that education was more than just learning math skills and how to read and write. We knew that by the time children were old enough to attend a CFC school they had already developed bad habits that contributed to malnourishment, disease, and poverty that were difficult to break, particularly if these bad habits were being reinforced in the home.

We started talking among ourselves about how nice it would be to have an impact on the children at a younger age, particularly if we could involve their parents. Huy Nareth, a government preschool coordinator in Spien Chrieve whose job it was to check on the welfare of the village children, told Savy and Kaye that she had identified four women in the village who were willing to offer their homes as a place for women and their preschool children to meet on a regular basis. At Kaye's urging, Nareth organized visits with Savy and Kaye so they could inspect each of the houses.

Only one home was really appropriate for a preschool, and even it was seriously battered, with ripped fleck sidings, plastic over the windows, a roof that was about to cave in, and an unsafe floor. A large family was also living there. Nevertheless, the owner of the house, the grandmother of the family, told us she was willing to open her home two or three times a week to any mother who wanted to come with her preschool kids. With stars in her eyes, Kaye asked Savy how much it would cost to renovate the shack.

"About $500," he told her.

Kaye took a few photographs of the dilapidated structure and emailed them to her former colleagues at SAS in Singapore. Christmas was only a few weeks away, so she didn't hold back as she pleaded her case. "This is a house that a kind family has offered to allow us to use a few days a week for a preschool," she wrote. "How about you rattle your pockets and give to a collection so that we can renovate it and make it safe? We need just $500 to make it wonderful."

Kaye's husband George was collecting the donations and he called her that night to tell her, "I think you are going to get your wish. We have $230 in the pot already!"

The next morning Kaye emailed her list again, thanking them and writing, "We are halfway to being able to rebuild this little house. Thank you so much, but if you can rattle your pockets again, we can make it happen."

George called her a few hours later with the news: "Kaye, we have $5,000.

See what I mean about our volunteers in Singapore? And this is a country that at that time was not very familiar with the idea of public service. Thanks to the generosity of those amazing folks CFC was able to completely rebuild the family's house and add a room that we filled with a blackboard and other supplies. We named it the Little Tree Preschool and it became a place where moms and their children could come together and learn.

Chang Rom, the same gentleman from the Ministry of Education who had been so enamored with our teacher training initiative, helped us with the red tape to get the preschool going. As part of his job, a year or so earlier he had tried to start a home-based preschool educational program in several villages, but the effort had failed, apparently because no one had been in charge of day-to-day operations at the individual sites. The good news was that this meant official documentation about teaching mothers and children in the home had already been created. Consequently, we had no pushback from the government about setting up our own home-based program, as long as we followed their guidelines.

On opening day we had thirteen moms and about the same number of children. Since this was a totally new concept to them, Savy, always the pragmatist, insisted we give the moms some kind of incentive to keep them coming. The tiniest of children were showing up wearing just a t-shirt or sometimes naked, so we started giving away free baby clothes, most of them donated by our community in Singapore.

Then Savy got the idea of giving something special to those moms who brought their kids in all week, usually tokens that could be exchanged for rice, clothing, or hygiene items.

One day during the first week or so, while Kaye was making an announcement about the rice and clothes, she heard giggles coming from

the back of the room. The somewhat embarrassed translator told her the mothers were wondering whether we might also provide them with bras and underwear.

Kaye mentioned this to one of our volunteers in Singapore, and amazingly not long afterwards a package arrived with dozens of new ladies briefs from Victoria's Secret. More giggles came when Kaye distributed them the following week, but they were giggles of appreciation.

We were hoping that once we got the moms to come to the preschool they would be hooked and inspired (and feel peer pressure) to stay with us. It worked, and the Little Tree Preschool was an immediate success. Suddenly mothers with common issues had a place where they could learn from each other and from the foreigner who had decided to move to Siem Reap to help educate their kids.

Unlike preschools in the States, moms at our preschools stay with their children, since our program is as much for them as it is for their kids. Most of the young mothers were reared by moms of the Khmer Rouge generation, so they have no role models. They reached motherhood with no idea of the skills needed to raise healthy, inspired children. Our preschool teachers are constantly prodding the mothers to think differently by asking them questions like:

- What can you do to develop your child's language and reasoning abilities?
- What can you do to build physical agility and strength in your toddlers?
- How do you care for your child socially and emotionally?
- What are ways to reach specific benchmarks that define healthy, happy babies?
- What help do you need to reach these goals?

Sometimes our focus is on simple skills like breastfeeding or bathing young babies, tasks that new moms in most countries take for granted. A simple thing like giving a toddler a toy to distract him while he takes a bath is a revelation to them.

Part of Kaye's preschool "curriculum" encourages the moms to look at picture books with their kids and to include them in household activities like cooking and putting toys away. Sometimes more serious discussions occur too, like the importance of talking to and hugging their children and comforting them when they are upset or want attention. Kaye even found herself teaching communications skills moms could use to deal with alcoholic husbands, a big problem in some villages.

By the middle of the school year Little Tree was overflowing and we began looking for a site where we could open a second preschool. We liked the safe, nurturing environment of Little Tree, housed as it was in someone's home, and we sought to replicate that elsewhere. We put out the word, and soon So Sopea, our Cambodian staff person in charge of our teacher training center and Food for Thought programs, pointed us to a mushroom farm right behind his family home. The farmer had become Sopea's surrogate father after his dad passed away, and we convinced him to offer us the concrete room where the mushrooms were stored.

We fixed it up and called this second preschool the Mushroom House. It too was an instant success, and the enthusiasm among new moms prompted us to open several more preschools in short order. Since then we have also added rooms in existing CFC schools to accommodate additional preschool programs.

As Little Tree Preschool's first anniversary approached, Kaye asked the mothers how they wanted to commemorate it. They suggested that instead of a party, what they wanted more than anything was a ride in our CFC van.

Consequently, on the preschool's first anniversary we piled as many people as we could into the van and the overflow into a couple of rented trucks and took the moms and their children on a picnic to Boray, a water reservoir with a beautiful, expansive view of the countryside. This picnic has since become an annual Little Tree Preschool tradition.

Early in 2008 Kaye hired Huy Nareth as full-time coordinator of our preschool program. She had already worked as both a teacher and a preschool administrator for the local government and was also a veteran of our teacher training sessions, so she was truly the perfect person for the job. A strong woman with a can-do attitude and a heart that warmed students and mothers alike, Nareth in many way became the matriarch of the CFC family, and her sudden death in December 2012 was a terrible tragedy for all of us. Not big on talk and generally reserved, her sense of pride and hope for her country was nevertheless inspiring.

Born in Phnom Penh in 1958, Nareth was the third of seven children. Her father was an equestrian at the Royal Palace, performing jumps and participating in parades for the king. Nareth even traveled with him to France a couple of times. He passed away in 1961 when Nareth was three, not much older than many of her current preschool students.

When the Khmer Rouge invaded Phnom Penh in 1975 Nareth fled to Siem Reap with her mother and siblings. Her education cut short, she was forced to farm and build canals. After the fall of the Khmer Rouge, her mother arranged for her to marry, and in 1979 Nareth moved with her new husband, Tiv Koul, to Tonle Sap Lake, where they sold fish and fresh vegetables. Their marriage was a happy one and together they raised four children. Sadly, Tiv passed away in 2005.

Encouraged by a family member to become a teacher, Nareth was accepted into the teacher training college program in Phnom Penh. In the classroom she regained the confidence that had been eroded during the Khmer Rouge years, and for years she passed that confidence on to new generations of Cambodians.

Our preschool program has been one of CFC's greatest successes, empowering the women who regularly attend to feel good about themselves as women, wives, and mothers. We also see a huge difference in the children compared to those who enter a CFC kindergarten or first grade classroom without having attended preschool. Not surprisingly, those who have already experienced a preschool environment are much better prepared to stay focused in class and to participate in interactive learning.

Thanks to sponsorship by the logistics company Agility, we've been able to double our number of preschools to twelve. We are still giving away baby clothes and rice, but ladies' underwear, not so much.

Kaye Made a Difference

I don't know that I have ever admired anyone more than I do Kaye Bach. During her two years in Siem Reap, CFC really came of age, and the impact of her constant presence convinced us we would always need a full-time CFC teacher trainer on the ground in Cambodia. In fact, when she finally moved back to Singapore, it left a giant hole, although we were fortunate to find Megan Smith to become our in-country deputy director in Siem Reap. Megan doesn't have Kaye's teacher training experience, but she is fantastic at rolling up her sleeves and taking on many jobs, including coordinating all our volunteer trips, our HR needs in Cambodia, and being our eyes and ears on the ground in Siem Reap.

Beyond Kaye's unique contributions to CFC, something magical happened between us. We became friends and confidants, connecting on a special level. Her husband George reminds me of Bill in the way he supports and guides her, and while there is no doubt that Ms. Bach is her own strong-willed lady, she relies on George's advice much as I do on Bill's.

Kaye and I have shared numerous orange moments, as well as inspirational cards we call "Today I will" cards. For example, a card might read, "Today I will look at the world through the eyes of a child" or "Today I will accept that God has given me a challenge with a lesson in it."

I began to share my deepest thoughts with Kaye. Sometimes I felt like my job and my life were overwhelming, but then I would look at Kaye living in Siem Reap full time and realize that her challenges were greater than mine. Our mutual words of encouragement and inspiration became part of our conversations, our emails, and our ESP.

Kaye was funny about the "God" thing. I knew God had put me in this position and Kaye in hers, but Kaye just believed it was because of a higher "something." There were times during Kaye's two years in Siem Reap when I could not sleep because of the challenges I was dealing with in Singapore or with Austin, but knowing she had left her family and a better paying job in Singapore to move to Siem Reap made me want to work even harder. There were many times when I asked myself, "Can I really do this?"

I never said "I can't," but I was always "asking." Then I would think of people like Kaye who had given up their cushy comforts to help those in need and boom! Nothing could slow me down. My question was constantly being answered and I knew I could not and would not give up.

Kaye left an indelible mark on everyone she touched within the CFC family. She developed deep relationships with the teachers, the children, their parents, and her colleagues, particularly Savy.

That latter bond was sealed even tighter during the summer of 2011 when Kaye and George took a long-planned holiday to Vietnam. They had already visited Ho Chi Minh City (Saigon) and the southern part of the country and were on their way to the beautiful north, including Hanoi and Halong Bay, when they received word that Savy's wife Mum was in the maternity ward at Ho Chi Minh City Hospital, about to have their first baby.

The prospective parents were far from their families, all alone, and not a little scared, so Kaye and George turned around and returned to Ho Chi Minh City. They drove straight to the hospital and found Savy in the waiting room, pacing nervously, very glad to see them.

Savy and Mum have lived a real love story. They first met when Mum was seventeen and a student in Savy's English class at the rundown school in Spien Chrieve. Savy says, "The first time I saw her she stopped my heart."

Like Savy, Mum had grown up very poor. Her parents divorced when she was three weeks old and she was pretty much raised by the community, particularly her next-door neighbors. She never knew her father, who had a half dozen or so wives, so Mum has half siblings all over Cambodia. Her father spent some time in jail in Thailand but ended up a successful businessman in Singapore, although they never had a relationship.

Mum had a cosmetics shop in the old market. Like a number of men in the village, Savy kept purchasing items from her shop as an excuse to see and talk to her. He told her they were for his sister, but she didn't buy that for a minute.

Mum's mother was none too happy about the growing relationship between her daughter and Savy, and was relieved when Mum received a marriage proposal from a man who came courting in a Land Cruiser. He lived in a large house and was offering a handsome dowry, but Mum refused him, only to receive another proposal a few months later from a government official.

Despite continuing pressure from her family, she refused him too. Savy and Mum were in love, and she was adamant that she wanted to stay single, since Savy didn't yet have the money for them to marry. Her relatives were angry, but Mum didn't care.

Savy's parents were none too happy either. They had hoped Savy would marry into a well-off family too.

Finally in 2000 the young couple had saved $800 between them and they announced their engagement.

Mum's mother was furious and refused to allow them to have the wedding in her home as was traditional. In fact, both families threatened to boycott the ceremony. It seemed the entire village was against them, but Savy and Mum called their bluff. The day before the wedding, both parents finally gave in and agreed to participate.

Each of the four hundred guests brought a donation to help pay for the wedding, but after all the bills were paid Savy and Mum had just $10 left over.

For the first year of their marriage the couple lived with Mum's mother. Mum's shop wasn't going well and she had to close it, but Savy was working regularly as a tour guide and tutoring young children in English, so they were eventually able to move into a small apartment.

Ten years later, after many efforts to have a child, Mum was finally expecting their first. I consider it a miracle that she finally got pregnant. She had undergone in vitro fertilization in Vietnam, so they decided to have the delivery there as well, but they found the hospital's waiting room in Ho Chi Minh City as bad as anything in Cambodia, with patients lying side by side, bleeding, moaning, and suffering.

Fortunately, the maternity ward was a bit better. Kaye and George arrived the same day Mum's C-section was scheduled and were able to sit with Savy and assure him that everything was going to be okay. Then they joined the new parents in welcoming their magnificent son, Ung Dawson, into this very orange world.

After this experience how could Kaye not return to us full-time? Sure enough, she is now back in Singapore, the head of our Education Committee and our liaison with Lehigh University.

NINE

Indelible Orange

To this day, I am still like a child on Christmas morning every time I get off the plane in Siem Reap, knowing I am about to enter the orange magic of Caring for Cambodia. That's definitely what I was feeling early in 2009 when Savy and I set off to do reconnaissance for what we hoped would be our next CFC school in the village of Aranh.

While it is only a ten-minute drive from the Amelio School in Spien Chrieve, Aranh provokes a much different feeling. At the Amelio School you walk outside the school gates and are in the heart of the village. Aranh, by contrast, is much more rural. On one side are poor families living in dilapidated, often one-room homes, but the other three directions provide magnificent vistas. Look one way and you see a classic Buddhist monastery; turn left or right and you are looking at farmland and rice paddies stretching as far as the eye can see.

Both Savy and Kaye were lobbying for our next school to be in Aranh. Savy had fond memories of the village because it was where he had first taught English after moving to Siem Reap, and Kaye had helped several Aranh teachers matriculate through our teacher training program. These were the teachers to whom she had made the promise a year earlier that if all went well, they would be part of CFC someday.

That someday was now.

I didn't need much convincing, but you had to look beneath the surface to actually be impressed with the situation in Aranh. The school's physical condition was terrible, probably the worst we had yet encountered. The campus was basically a continuation of the neighboring rice paddies, and the beat-up cement building had no floor to speak of and a roof that had been almost completely torn off. No wonder the dropout rate was so high. Who would want to go to school there?

By 2009 the situation had reached a crisis, with enrollment at an all-time low of fewer than two hundred children. It didn't help that family dynamics often discouraged attendance. Children in Aranh begin helping their families in the rice paddies at a very young age and school simply ceases to be a priority.

Despite these difficulties, our experience at our other schools helped us imagine what a new building and a cleaned-up campus would look like. Savy and Kaye also sensed something special about the village and the people who lived there. Historically, the school's proximity to the main road, which made both students and teachers familiar with the influence of western tourists, had given them a sort of sophistication, or at least a recognition that there was a larger world beyond their own. The important role the monastery played in the community also contributed to a strong, if currently latent, commitment to education.

According to Savy, the K–6 school in Aranh had been thriving until about ten years earlier when teachers had stopped being paid regularly and students had begun to drop out or not show up at all. Attendance had plummeted from a high of more than five hundred students, and the teachers lacked any clear sense of direction.

Fortunately, we did have the support of some key individuals within the community. These included the teachers who had participated in our training sessions and the principal, who enthusiastically talked to Savy, Kaye, and me about replicating the successes we'd had in Spien Chrieve and Bakong. We also had an advocate in Suy Larm, one of the important elders of the community who later became chairman of the local PTA.

For these community leaders and a number of the parents the thought of having a new school building was the end of the rainbow. But we envisioned many additional possibilities—a renovated school building, yes, but also enough room for a cafeteria, a water filtration system, bathrooms with inside plumbing, and even a CFC administrative office. We even dreamt of a campus that could expand in three directions, ultimately with an elementary, junior high, and high school that would make it possible for students to matriculate straight through from kindergarten to the twelfth grade.

That was *our* dream: for the first time, maybe in Aranh, children could receive a continuous CFC education. We even pictured students going off to college or vocational school and then on to careers more varied than tuk-tuk drivers or tour guides. This was our goal—to prepare our students for life after CFC.

Before committing to the school in Aranh, however, Savy and I agreed that we first wanted to see the teachers and administrators demonstrate their own commitment to significant improvements in both attitude and performance. This meant Savy was a frequent visitor to Aranh in the months before we formally agreed to adopt it, and whenever I was in Siem Reap I accompanied him.

The first time we entered the existing school building together we found a crumbling foundation and rubbish lying everywhere, with most of the classrooms emitting a foul smell. The school had no lock and we suspected kids were breaking in during school holidays.

Savy told the principal we would return soon and that we hoped our next visit would find the trash picked up and the classrooms looking, feeling, and smelling fresher.

On our next visit the school did look much better. The principal was clearly making an effort and asking for our help. This time he promised that the teachers would start showing up more regularly, and that too began to happen.

In response, we agreed to begin by repairing the school's doors and windows. At the same time, Savy, Kaye, and I sat down with the principal and explained our regular strategy:

- Shore up the foundation of the school building.
- Repair the roof.
- Tile the classroom floors.
- Paint the school inside and out.
- Augment teacher salaries as teachers commit to being punctual and to foregoing any under-the-table payments from the students.
- Train the teachers.
- Implement our health and hygiene initiatives along with our Food for Thought program.

Eventually Mr. San and his crew renovated the long, one-story building into six separate classrooms and began construction on a new two-story building. As always, we worked with community leaders and Cambodia's Ministry of Education to get all the approvals we needed. We then installed a water filtration system and toilets, along with a teacher resource center, library, and cafeteria. None of this could have been accomplished without the generous support of our Singapore community, particularly the McCabe and Leonard families, who continue to give without any desire for recognition.

At the start of the semester our Food for Thought program was ready to feed every child twice a day, and on the first day of school we distributed uniforms and backpacks to every student. Morale began to improve even before our teacher training sessions began. Aranh today is thriving, mainly because we were able to quickly put in place the lessons we had learned at our other schools.

Thinking Long-Term

Bill and I were constantly brainstorming about different ways CFC might continue to expand. Simultaneously we pondered how to ensure the organization's more widespread, sustainable success. We were making a powerful difference in the lives of thousands of children and their families in Siem Reap, yet CFC was still only touching a small fraction of the Cambodian school population.

With his CEO background, Bill taught me to focus on the end game, which was to make CFC "sustainable and scalable." This meant eliminating the need for constant fundraising by making CFC self-sufficient, as well as scaling our efforts across the country.

We wanted our standards of education to become the de facto standards for K–12 education across Cambodia, with the ultimate objective of handing over operational responsibilities to the communities of Siem Reap. In short, our goal was for every Cambodian community to have clean schools, trained teachers who were paid on time, and healthy children.

In order to make the successes we were having permanent and a model that would be followed by schools across Cambodia, we needed to be able to quantify the results of our efforts and to step up our fundraising. These two goals were intertwined, since funders want to see both past results and future projections.

Anecdotally we knew we were doing a lot of good and improving the lives of many, many children. Anyone who had visited one of our schools before our involvement and then again a year later could attest to the dramatic differences we were making, but so far we had no way to measure that success. We had plenty of questions, but no definitive way to answer them. What impact were we actually having on people's lives? Were students at our schools healthier than those at non-CFC schools? Were children getting a better education at CFC schools, and if so, would this make a difference in their lives once they left school and, hopefully, entered the workforce?

How could we analyze statistically what we had accomplished? How could we gather and use the data to demonstrate our successes to potential funders and to the Cambodian government?

At our CFC board meetings we began talking about ways to assess the progress we had made so far to determine what was working and what was not, and to set goals for the next decade and beyond.

At this point the CFC leadership team consisted of Natalie Bastow and Paige Okun in Singapore, Savy and Kaye in Siem Reap, and Bill and me. We also received tremendous support from our remarkable board of directors, people like Chris Graves, Michael O'Neill, and Cuong Do. Cuong, now senior vice president of corporate strategy and business development at TE Connectivity, has continually kept us on the straight and narrow when it comes to focusing on the long term. He is the leading advocate on our board for creating an endowment fund as a way to sustain our efforts.

Natalie Bastow, COO.

Christy Machulski, Anne Wilhoit, Patty Spooner at a Caring Tea. Below is one of Michele Smith's beautiful tables.

CFC "A" team at our Caring Tea 2010.

Egg-a-thon.

Solita Miller, Avery and Bill at an Egg-a-thon.

An ArtAid working trip to Siem Reap. Heloiza Montuori, Stephanie Randall, Sandra Smith, Blair Speciale, and Pen Rithy with CFC students.

Food for Thought.

Students eating a breakfast of rice porridge with veggies and meat.

Top students receiving bicycles—transportation for the whole family sometimes.

The Aranh-Cuthbert Junior High School opening with His Excellency, Um Sithy, Minister of Education.

Hope Bartolotta, Ambassador Sichan Siv, his wife, Martha Patrillo Siv, and me in Siem Reap, 2011. Susan Mars, and Narin Jamison, Liz King and me in DC.

The Edds Family—Carolyn, Teal, Catherine, Andrew, Nathaniel. Daughter Anna is not in the photo.

Kristie Hess, CFO.

Kaye celebrating our first CFC Day with Chea Sophea's daughter, Voleak.

The late Nareth and Savy with preschool mothers and kids.

Samedi with his son, So Sapha, on his first day of kindergarten at Kong Much school; he's now in the first grade.

Megan Smith, Deputy Country Manager, and Diane Ayres, Director of Teacher Training. Both reside in Siem Reap.

Austin (l) taking Polaroids of Cambodian children at the Bakong temple; he gave the photos to the kids. Anthony (r) with first graders at the Amelio school.

Top row (l-r), Kelley Trcka, Tiffany Milco, me (seven months pregnant w Avery), Debby Lemiuex. Bottom, my sister, Valorie Parker, and Virginia.

Cherry in second grade at the Amelio school.

Avery and I getting ready for her dance recital. Making memories.

Bill and his girls—Rathana, Cherry, Avery and me.

Savy, Mum and Dawson.

Austin's graduation from St. Edwards University, 2011.

A Partnership with Lehigh

Another place we turned to for help was Lehigh University. Bill had attended Lehigh on a wrestling scholarship and was an active alumnus; he delivered the 2008 commencement address. Just as we were getting started in Aranh he made a trip to Lehigh in Bethlehem, Pennsylvania, to meet with a group of administrators and professors to brainstorm about the possibility of a partnership between Lehigh and CFC.

We figured both organizations had a lot to gain. Bill and I liked the idea of making a significant contribution to Lehigh while at the same time taking advantage of their academic expertise to help us measure our successes and plan a strategy that would fulfill our long-term goals.

We wanted Lehigh to identify and prepare funding grants and to quantify our successes so that this data could be included in grant proposals. We also hoped that by incorporating CFC into Lehigh's graduate curriculum we would be the beneficiary of some needed manpower in Siem Reap from smart people committed to working in a developing country.

As for Lehigh, the partnership would be a creative way to further internationalize its curriculum and advance its footprint through internationally recognized research and unique student experiences. The school was always looking for ways to give students meaningful encounters beyond taking classes or conducting research in a foreign country but inside an American bubble. Students who worked with CFC would have the opportunity to tackle real-world solutions to the most basic problems found in developing countries.

Bill and I agreed to fund a series of graduate courses at Lehigh that would explore the theoretical approaches to understanding the role of education in international development, but also train graduate students to conduct evaluations specific to CFC. This would include on-campus training in the United States, as well as practical, hands-on data collection in Siem Reap so that students could see for themselves the reality of Cambodian education.

Ultimately, Lehigh graduate students interviewed CFC staff and volunteers, teachers, and people in the community at all of our schools, as well as representatives of a number of other NGOs. Part of the curriculum involved examining what other organizations, including the United Nations, the World Bank, and NGOs and state agencies, were doing that might complement or conflict with CFC's agenda. The backdrop to these courses was the devastation of Cambodia's educational system caused by the Khmer Rouge and the impact that continues to linger.

Subsequent visits by the graduate students began to investigate how well our child-centered schools were preparing students for employment. Graduate students also met with various stakeholders in the Siem Reap labor market and interviewed some of the major employers in the area, as well as CFC faculty and staff. They also began project evaluations of CFC activities like Food for Thought, our health and hygiene initiatives, our preschools, and our clean water efforts.

Just spending time in the communities, soaking up the atmosphere and learning a bit about Cambodian culture, gave the students insight into a mindset completely different from their own. At one of our community meetings, a graduate student asked the Spien Chrieve community leader about the general health of the villagers.

"We don't have any health problems," he replied sincerely, while the Westerners saw with their own eyes malnourishment and disease all around them.

At the local level at least, many Cambodians do not realize there is any reality beyond sick kids and people dying prematurely. They are just accustomed to a different kind of normal. That is the status quo CFC is trying to change.

In the fall of 2011 Lehigh University hired Dr. Sothy Eng as its international education professorship of practice, a position spelled out in the partnership agreement. We had been looking for someone with expertise in early childhood education who had some experience in a developing country and who understood Cambodia in particular.

This was a thin needle to thread, and we felt fortunate when Dr. Eng applied for the job. He grew up near Phnom Penh during the Khmer Rouge regime but emigrated to the United States, where he received his M.S. and Ph.D. in Human Development and Family Development from Texas Tech University.

The entire program was led by Dr. Iveta Silova, program director of Lehigh's Comparative and International Education Department, another woman who turned orange. From the very start, she was committed to making the Lehigh/CFC partnership a success.

Dreaming of More

Our K–6 schools had rapidly become outstanding, a model for the rest of Cambodia, but reaching older students was more challenging. Dropout rates, particularly after grade six, were high. Even if young people did continue their studies, finding work after graduating high school was difficult. This created a vicious cycle that revolved around the following question: why get an education if it wasn't going to improve your life or that of your family?

We needed to make the value of education self-fulfilling. If younger students saw that those who made it through high school had better jobs than dropouts, they too would be encouraged to stay in school.

Our dream of giving students the opportunity to matriculate from kindergarten through high school was realized at the end of 2012 with the opening of the high school in Aranh. Up until this point our only experience with high school was in Bakong. Back in 2006 Cambodia's Ministry of Education had spent months trying to persuade us to take Bakong High School under our wing, but I had been reluctant. On the one hand, the idea of extending our influence on a child's life all the way through high school was compelling. One of our foundational goals was to create an infrastructure that would help children go from preschool to high school and graduate with a promising future.

On the other hand, I had felt that Bakong High School was at that time more than we could handle. If we were going to take on the responsibility for a child's entire pre-college education, we were going to need new curriculum for the older grades, new teacher training materials and expertise, and a new focus on life after CFC. That was a lot to tackle just a few years after opening our first school in Spien Chrieve.

Complicating matters was that Hun Sen Bakong High School was a special project of Cambodia's prime minister. He had built it and named it after himself. We feared that if we adopted it like we had our other schools, we would become mired in politics that would compromise our reputation as an independent guide to better education.

A walk through the high school only increased my concerns. From the outside the building seemed in decent condition, but once inside we walked into uninspired classrooms with cobwebs on the ceiling, cement floors, and the traditional "chalk and talk" method of teaching. Teacher absenteeism was a huge problem, and some unusual political issues soon became apparent.

Normally when I tour a school I constantly grill the teachers and even the students. I am rarely reticent about asking whatever questions come to mind, but this time Savy admonished me to hold my tongue and to voice any questions I had to him in private.

"We'll talk about it later," he warned me every time I started to mouth off. Since he had already told me this was Prime Minister Hun Sen's school, I definitely got the picture.

That picture came into fuller view a few months later after we had tentatively agreed to become involved. I had often wondered about the always-empty room in one of the buildings at the far end of campus. One day we noticed that seemingly out of nowhere someone had installed dozens of small desks and what must have been close to a hundred sewing machines. Savy thought that maybe they were going to be used for vocational education training, but something did not seem right. Then Savy learned that the wife of a top official in the Cambodian government had plans to use high school students to make clothing that we assumed would then be sold at a profit, most likely in Phnom Penh.

This was nothing short of free child labor and it tapped right back into my feeling of unease during my first trip to Cambodia when I saw those young women being exploited in the Red Light district.

I knew we had to stand up and do the right thing. After numerous conversations with Savy, Bill and I made it clear to Cambodia's Ministry of Education that CFC could not have anything to do with child labor. The school could, of course, use the sewing machines any way it chose, but in that case we would pull out of our relationship with the high school, which at that point hadn't begun in earnest. To our relief, the sewing machines suddenly disappeared as mysteriously as they had arrived.

The removal of the sewing machines notwithstanding, Bakong High School was a challenge from the start. Part of the problem was that some of the techniques that had worked so well in our primary schools were a harder sell in the more crowded, more jaded environment of a high school. High school teachers are paid more, so our monthly stipend of $5 or even $10 didn't mean as much as it did in the primary schools. And even more than in Aranh, the students, because they were older, were more valuable to their families as farm workers, guides, or to hawk souvenirs.

Nevertheless, conditions at Bakong High School slowly began to improve once some of the same strategies we had applied in the lower grades began to take hold. A project called "Operation Cleanup" was a big success, with students, teachers, and administrators pitching in for a major campus cleanup. We repainted several buildings, cleaned out most of the classrooms, and installed new desks. Perhaps our proudest achievement was the new, well-stocked library, which gradually became an ongoing resource for students in all grades. During the 2010–'11 school year students paid 53,912 student visits to the library.

How do I know the exact number? Cambodians tend to be overly diligent about record keeping, a remnant from the horrors of the Khmer Rouge. The teachers kept a jar by the library door and students dropped in a stone each time they entered. At the end of the day the librarian counted the stones.

We also gradually began to get buy-in from more and more of the high school teachers. Adapting a teacher training program specifically for them definitely helped, as did follow-up support by our mentor teachers.

Two Junior High Schools

While high schools remain a challenge for CFC and a continuing area of focus, our efforts have been helped by edging closer to that age group with our successes at two junior high schools, one in Aranh and the other in Bakong.

We targeted Aranh as the site of our first junior high school mainly because our primary school there had become a big success so quickly. By the third month after opening its doors, almost half the teachers had attended at least one teacher training session and most of the others were about to follow suit. At the same time, MAD trip volunteers, directed by CFC staff, had made a variety of campus improvements, including the installation of a safe and brightly colored playhouse, a new swing set, and a hand-painted Caring for Cambodia emblem that the staff proudly placed above the windows.

The volunteers also remodeled the CFC office with bright colors to make it child friendly and a more inviting place for teachers, staff, and visitors. Part of the group, led by Marc L'Heureux, the vice principal at SAS for the primary grades, even rebuilt the barber shop owned by Suy Larm, the community leader, with Marc's entire family chipping in.

Another of my favorite projects was building a new gravel driveway so students no longer lost their shoes in the mud on their way to class. Our volunteers from Singapore worked alongside Cambodian students like an old-time fire brigade, passing baskets of gravel, six tons in all, hand to hand from trucks to the new driveway.[7]

By the end of 2009 the number of students enrolled at the primary school in Aranh had more than doubled to 546 children. Now we wanted sixth grade graduates to have an equally fine junior high school, which meant figuring out a way to pay for the construction of a brand new building.

Once again, unexpected angels appeared. Peter and Alison Cuthbert were both teachers at SAS whose interest in Cambodia predated CFC and who were now generous supporters. On one of our teacher training trips Peter spoke with Kaye about getting more involved. We immediately took him up on the offer and he, along with another teacher from SAS, initiated a training program for high school teachers.

On one of these trips Peter mentioned to Kaye that his parents were looking to build a school in South Africa. Kaye replied, "Why there and

---

7. The driveway was washed away during the 2011 floods, then rebuilt in 2012.

not here?" Peter and Ally suggested to his parents that for a relatively modest donation they could make a huge impact on hundreds of children in Siem Reap. After a lot of back and forth emailing George and Wendy Cuthbert agreed to pay for the construction of a junior high school in Aranh. It became a labor of love for the entire community as well as for Mr. San and his construction crew, dozens of MAD volunteers, and the CFC staff.

As three floors went up, the villagers watched the construction with pride and then pitched in to create a beautiful flower garden and to install planters that now hang from the second floor balconies. They also helped paint the building and each classroom, truly claiming the school as their own.

The three-story school building, an unusual structure for Siem Reap, became our proudest physical achievement, housing a dozen classrooms, a modern cafeteria, a computer and science lab, and a well-stocked library. The official opening took place at the end of February, 2011. Decorations adorned the entire campus, while hundreds of spectators, including government officials, CFC's board of directors, and Peter Cuthbert representing the Cuthbert family, watched traditional Apsara dancers and a marching band herald the opening.

His Excellency Im Sethy, Cambodia's minister of education, presided and said some kind words about CFC's impact on Cambodian education. He also gave the Golden Hand Award to three of CFC's most valuable people, Christy Miller, Kaye Bach, and Katie Sansom. This very special award is given by the Cambodian government to people who have worked to help rebuild Cambodia.

I have yet to meet George and Wendy Cuthbert, but a month after the official opening they visited Siem Reap to participate in a second ceremony, a blessing by local monks. Three generations of Cuthberts were in attendance, as well as village officials, CFC staff, and four hundred smiling, enthusiastic schoolchildren.

George and Wendy Cuthbert at the Aranh Cuthbert Junior High School opening ceremony.

The Aranh Cuthbert Junior High School is more than just a beautiful new building. Since the day its doors opened, students from the primary schools in Aranh, Spien Chrieve, and Kong Much have been taught in a specialized learning environment with motivated teachers. The campus hums each day with energetic students and devoted teachers. It has become a flagship school for the nation. Cambodia's Ministry of Education calls it a model for progressive education.

One of the school's innovations is that students move from classroom to classroom, taking different subjects with different teachers. No one in Siem Reap had ever heard of anything like that before, and when we started doing it in a limited way in our primary schools we had to get the approval of the Ministry of Education. The kids loved it, and it has now become the norm in all our upper grades.

CFC's second junior high school is located in Bakong. As in Aranh, after completing the sixth grade, many of the children in Bakong are expected to help support their families and are particularly vulnerable to dropping out of school. We began to dream a little, looking for funding to build a junior high school there. Through a bit of serendipity and another school connection to one of my own children, we succeeded.

During another "What do your parents do?" show-and-tell at Avery's preschool in Singapore in 2009, I described CFC and what we were doing in Siem Reap. Avery's friend Zahra Motwani was taken with the presentation. In the days that followed I got to know her mother, Anjna, who expressed an interest in helping CFC. Anjna became a valuable volunteer, and a few months later she and her husband Sanjay wanted to discuss the idea of funding a school. Similar to the Cuthberts, they had been running into red tape while trying to support early childhood education in India.

Thanks to the incredible generosity of the Motwanis, construction began on the school in the spring of 2011, and a few months later they traveled from Singapore to participate in the groundbreaking and blessing ceremony of the Bakong Motwani Junior High School.

Sanjay, Anjna and Sarina Motwani at the groundbreaking for Motwani Junior High School. Two of their children, Zahra and Krish, are not in the photo.

206

More than four hundred students now attend our two junior high schools and we have added more teacher training sessions aimed specifically at teachers in these grades.

In the fall of 2011, to coincide with the opening of the junior high in Bakong, we hired Diane Ayres, a middle school teacher at the Tanglin Trust School and a familiar face on CFC teacher training trips, as our new director of teacher training in Siem Reap. She works with our mentor teachers to develop teaching strategies and resources aimed specifically at the junior high school level. In November of 2011 she coordinated our first teacher training session for CFC's secondary school teachers.

For many of these teachers, this two-and-a-half-day teacher training session, conducted by five teachers from SAS, was their first introduction to creating a lesson plan and presenting material in a way that encouraged students to become more active in the learning process. Once again, our goal was to move teachers away from the old "chalk and talk" method that was so ingrained in their own educational experiences, and we found that most of the teachers were eager to teach in a different way.

Challenges and Solutions

As CFC has matured, one of our central goals has become preparing our students for meaningful employment and active citizenship within their communities. The Lehigh research has helped us quantify the considerable challenges we face. Specifically, we have learned that:

- Students have a respect for education but lack the finances to complete secondary school.
- Students are not informed about where to look for jobs or what skills they need in order to secure jobs.
- Many jobs require a certain level of English proficiency that most students do not possess.

- The main areas of economic growth in Cambodia are tourism, banking, technology, organic farming, and fishing, all of which require specialized skills and training and none of which are being taught in the public school system, including our schools.
- Students at Bakong High School are unprepared to enter the Siem Reap workforce and generally have no experience filling out a job application, creating a resume, or interviewing for a job, much less actually having a job.
- When high school graduates do manage to find employment, turnover rates are high because they do not understand the culture of the workforce environment (i.e., new hires are frequently late or absent and show little enthusiasm for their jobs, behavior that is similar to the behavior of teachers at Siem Reap schools prior to CFC's involvement).

These realities were sobering, but they also spurred us to follow through on a number of initiatives already underway at Bakong High School, including developing internships with local businesses and networking with CFC alumni, as well as continuing four important projects we had adopted by the fall of 2011:

- Building a career resource center where students could find job-seeking resources such as sample resumes, interview techniques, and a job board.
- Creating a work study program to give students work experience.
- Offering life skills training backed by teacher training.
- Offering curriculum and teacher training relevant to the skills high school students would need after graduating.

Career Corner

In 2011 we established "Career Corner" at Bakong High School. This is a place where students can find an ever-changing job board and information on local training schools, universities, sample resumes and cover letters, company brochures, and salary and wage information.

Here students learn the "how to's" of applying for a job, including creating a resume, filling out applications, preparing for interviews, improving communication skills, and gaining confidence and knowledge about the job-seeking process, concepts that were unknown to Cambodian students or to their parents. An orientation program by CFC staff teaches students how to use the Career Corner and has created a system for tracking usage.

We've had a lot of help from Bakong High School faculty, who were very involved in the planning and implementation of the Career Corner. Student council members have been active too, helping their peers learn about educational and employment opportunities, while at the same time gaining valuable work experience themselves by facilitating these sessions.

Having Hillary Vance join us full time in Siem Reap as our secondary schools program manager has also boosted these efforts. Hillary, who studied Khmer at the Center for Khmer Studies in Phnom Penh, has a master's degree from Lehigh University in Globalization and Educational Change and a certificate in International Development in Education. She is in charge of the Career Corner and our work study and internship programs and is developing projects at Bakong High School specifically aimed at preparing graduates for the workforce or for higher education. Recently, for example, she organized a career day that gave students the opportunity to meet local businessmen. A big crowd was in attendance, boosted by the lunch we served, and we're working on ways to improve similar future events.

For example, we've already created resources in the Khmer language related to jobs and university opportunities. We've found that posters with pictures and simple explanations is an effective way to present message points, such how to dress for a job interview.

We have also established a work study program that begins with having students apply and interview for unpaid jobs at Bakong High School. Just the experience of applying for a job has proven invaluable, since even students who are not selected benefit from writing a resume and going through the interview process.

The jobs themselves teach students important skills too. A number of students work at the Career Corner, helping other students use the resources, write cover letters and resumes, and apply for jobs or entry into college or vocational schools. Other students in the work study program learn how to organize the library or help out in the office. We hope these jobs will help students begin to understand the professionalism needed to succeed in the workforce and the responsibilities required to complete everyday tasks.

Meanwhile, CFC is also working to develop a network of safe, trusted local companies willing to offer internships to our upperclassmen.

Life Skills

In the past if you asked our students what they wanted to be when they grew up, many would say tour guides, farmers, taxi drivers, or in a few cases, teachers. In recent years the list has become much more varied. We now have kids who dream about being scientists, professors, artists, world leaders, and pop stars. As these dreams stir, we want to fortify our students with important life skills. For some that means learning the latest strategies in farming and fishing; for others it means exploring possibilities in local industries; for the top students it means preparing for university.

An emphasis on life skills has leaked into both our junior and high school curriculum and into our teacher training sessions. Subjects now include the vocational (small engine and bike repair), the practical (personal hygiene, gardening, raising fish), workplace readiness (learning English, becoming familiar with computers), cultural (Apsara dance, art, music, and photography), and civic (learning leadership skills through involvement in student council). In the spring of 2011, for example, secondary students created a vegetable garden on the Aranh campus and learned composting and other skills.

A beautiful example of success has been our ability to hire some of our own graduates. Suy Mealea, Seoum Sokheoun, Chum Kim Hong, and Kim Heim, all graduates from a CFC school, are now some of our best preschool teachers, while Som San is the English and computer teacher at the Aranh Cuthbert Junior High School.

TEN

Ten Years and Counting

2012 marked Caring for Cambodia's tenth year, counting from the day I stepped into the Kravaan classroom with Srelin. Please indulge this mother hen as I proudly rattle off some of the accomplishments of an organization run almost entirely by volunteers:

- Six thousand, four hundred students enrolled in sixteen CFC schools.
- One hundred and twenty-four CFC salaried staff on the ground in Cambodia.
- One hundred teachers trained through our teacher training program, including six Cambodian Ministry of Education employees who are now teacher trainers themselves.
- Twelve preschools with 196 children and 187 mothers.
- Thirteen kindergarten classes with 503 students.

- Five primary schools (grades one through six) with 84 teachers instructing 3,059 students.
- Two junior high schools and two senior highs instructing 2,081 students.
- Six libraries on our six different campuses, filled with thousands of books in both Khmer and English, donated by hundreds of families.
- One hundred and twenty thousand Food for Thought meals served every month.
- Thousands of bicycles bought and given away to CFC students and their families.
- Tens of thousands of toothbrushes and health and hygiene kits distributed to CFC children and their families.
- Fifty water wells and six large-scale water filtration systems installed (at least one per campus) and used by CFC students and their families, as well as by people from all over the villages.
- Twenty-two homes constructed by more than 700 CFC volunteers, who have also painted dozens of classrooms, educational buildings, offices, cafeterias, and libraries; built bulletin boards, bookshelves, and outside facades; cleaned fields and driveways; mounted world maps in all secondary school classrooms; and created gardens and playgrounds.
- Substantially higher promotion and graduation rates and substantially lower dropout rates than other schools in both Siem Reap and throughout Cambodia, according to research conducted by Lehigh University.

By now you understand that we started off as well-intentioned novices—expat women living in Singapore who would bring up what we were doing during dinner table talk with our husbands and families. Then on Mondays when our spouses went off to work (sometimes all across Asia) these amazing women would come together, and *continue* to come together to work for CFC.

Most of our husbands subsequently visited Siem Reap to see for themselves what it was all about, and once there they caught the orange bug too. In fact, many of them continue to be our staunchest supporters, evangelizing for CFC and providing enormous financial and in-kind help, often in the form of sweat equity on our Make A Difference trips.

Bill is *my* biggest supporter. When he's out of town, we typically talk several times a day and on the agenda is always our kids, the two of us, and CFC.

Our volunteer base has now expanded to hundreds of women and men from across the globe. Natalie Bastow, CFC's global chief operating officer, calls these individuals "the backbone of Caring for Cambodia," and they certainly are. Cumulatively they have spent thousands of hours volunteering, asking for nothing in return.

Students from Singapore on a Village Ramble with CFC students.

As the number of volunteers has swelled, so has the creativity of some of their activities. One of my favorites, which Kaye dubbed the Village Ramble, is a scavenger hunt that allows CFC students to practice their English while young volunteers get an insider's look at a Cambodian village as together they collect ordinary items like coconut shells, bamboo sticks, or prahok, a crushed, salted fermented fish paste that may not be so ordinary to volunteers from Europe, North America, or even Singapore.

Another popular activity that gets our volunteers together with our students are field trips, usually either to the national museum or to the temples, which, remarkably, many of our Cambodian students have never visited. One of our volunteers has prepared a question and answer sheet to enhance the learning experience for everyone.

The collection and distribution of clothing and school supplies has also expanded and become more organized. Each month we have a new priority, such as preschool clothes in January or teaching supplies in February.

Through our Kids Helping Kids program, elementary and secondary students from places as diverse as Pennsylvania, New Jersey, Washington DC, Florida, Hawaii, Seattle, Texas, Japan, Taiwan, and Switzerland regularly send donations to our distribution center in Singapore. These and other initiatives have allowed CFC to distribute tens of thousands of school uniforms, backpacks, pens, whiteboard markers, paper and pencils, and books.

One of our most recent initiatives began as a college tour to Phnom Penh for our most outstanding high school kids. Most of them had no idea what a college looked like.

Our people on the ground, including the principal at Bakong High, were initially skeptical. They didn't want kids to get excited about college only to realize they had no way to pay for it. My solution was to offer annual scholarships to up to ten high school seniors. The only requirement for consideration is to write a letter to CFC, explaining why they want to go to college. Tuition at Siem Reap University is only $680 per year, another example of how donations to CFC for college and vocational scholarships have a tremendous "bang for their buck." We're now making college and vocational school scholarships a centerpiece of our fundraising effort aimed at small donors.

Always Evolving CFC Leadership

One remarkable thing about the CFC volunteer organization in Singapore is the success and vibrancy it enjoys despite constant turnover. As I explained earlier, the expat community in Singapore is by its very nature transient, with people being rotated in and out of their corporate or diplomatic assignments after relatively short periods of time, typically two or three years. Bill and I were the exception, as we stayed for almost a decade.

In CFC's early years a key person's abrupt departure would leave a big hole in our system, but with so many people of all ages now depending on us, we can no longer afford a vacuum at the top of any of our key committees. Natalie solved this problem with a system for succession planning that ensures we always have more than one person who knows what's going on in every important area.

Thanks to technology that didn't exist ten years ago, we also find that many jobs can be performed just as easily from thousands of miles away as from around the corner. In 2011, for example, Laura Andrews, our communications director, moved with her family to Switzerland and hasn't missed a beat. From there she answers every email that comes through the CFC website and edits our eZine, *Voices from Siem Reap*, and our *Caring Connections*.

Likewise, Kristie Hess, now in Chicago, is still our CFO, and Cathy McNamara, who was co-chair of the Goods Donations Committee while in Singapore, helps Kristie with corporate matching from her home in Philadelphia. Martha Zeman, also in Chicago, regularly updates our Facebook page, Anna Deonanan does our graphics from North Carolina, and Eleni Scheidt, a former board member, ships our CFC logo items from Maryland.

Caring for Cambodia is now a truly international operation, with people working every day from all over the globe.

Some roles, of course, need to be performed in Singapore, so we will always have to replace people like our volunteer coordinator or our goods donations leader when they leave. The departure from Singapore of key volunteers is always sad, but fortunately CFC continues to attract new and equally dedicated replacements.

Operations Board

I think my departure from Singapore in 2010 challenged CFC to become more efficient and organized. As I was preparing my family for the move back to Texas, we restructured CFC so at the top we would have a more formal operations board made up of the women who lead our most important functions: Volunteer Coordination, Group Trip Planning, Communications, Health, Goods Donations, Food for Thought, and of course, the Education Committee.

Some of our most exciting recent initiatives have been run through our Health Committee, thanks largely to the new head of that group, Barbara Levy. Barbara arrived in Singapore from Massachusetts in August of 2008 with her two children, a dog, and two guinea pigs after her husband, a biomedical researcher, was sent to Singapore to work on a genome project, a joint venture between the National University of Singapore and Duke University in North Carolina.

Barbara's background is in hospital administration and psychiatry, and her story is typical for our key volunteers. Although she'd left the workforce to raise her children, once in Singapore she wanted to become involved in something worthwhile.

"I don't find it satisfying to just put a check in the mail," Barbara remembers. "CFC was different. The CFC community immediately made me feel welcome, and I started to talk with Natalie about my background and interests and how I might be able to help in a meaningful way."

CFC's Health Committee turned out to be a perfect fit. Early in 2010 Barbara joined Natalie and a few of our other volunteers on a trip to Siem Reap. Savin, Cherry's father and CFC's full-time nurse for all our schools, gave her a tour of the schools and his facilities, and she was hooked.

"Kaye's energy is also completely contagious," Barbara explains, "but it's the kids who really steal your heart. I came back wanting to help and with lots of ideas."

Her first idea was to reinforce what we were already doing. We had initiated a campaign to teach our CFC community in Siem Reap how the simple act of hand washing reduces the transmission of disease and saves lives, but Barbara took it to another level. She produced a large picture book that helped primary school teachers emphasize to their students the importance of clean hands and showed visually how easily germs spread from hand to mouth. The Health Committee followed up by making sure soap and water were available at all our schools, particularly near the bathrooms and where the children ate.

Sometimes solutions are so simple, but they still require someone to think about a given problem and follow through. When it turned out that most of our clean water stations had no place to rest a bar of soap, Barbara came up with the idea of a soap sock hung from a nail banged into the tile.

That worked fine for a while, and though the soap kept disappearing, we didn't mind. We figured kids were taking the soap home, where hopefully it was being put to good use. Now every teacher keeps extra bars on hand to dispense as needed.

Teeth brushing was already part of the kids' daily ritual, and "Wash, soap, rinse" now became part of it too. A renewed emphasis on the health of our students fit right in with our mission to go deep, not wide, in improving the lives of our CFC students. Each day we strive to ensure that our students are being taught well, but also that they are safe, well nourished, healthy, and clean. It's a straightforward plan: get the children healthy so they can become good students and teach them healthy habits that will hopefully ripple back to their families.

After her success with the soap socks, Barbara became more ambitious. Almost none of our students had ever had their eyes examined, so we persuaded doctors from the International Medical Clinic (IMC) in Singapore to travel to our CFC schools to perform eye exams. Russell Paul, IMC's general manager, became a great advocate for us among the other doctors at IMC. It also helped that we had a relationship with the Angkor Hospital for Children (AHC) in Siem Reap.

One day an American named Dr. Eugene Tragess (everyone called him Dr. Gene) came up to me in a bathing suit at the Raffles Hotel to offer his help. Dr. Gene was a surgery consultant at AHC and a heart surgery pioneer. He was married to a dynamic Cambodian woman, who became a pediatrician in 2011 shortly after Dr. Gene passed away. After his death, Dr. Varun Kumar, another American, agreed to continue Dr. Gene's work by allowing any of our students under the age of sixteen to be examined at the AHC eye clinic.

Relatively few of our students have actually needed glasses, perhaps because none of the kids in Siem Reap play video games, or perhaps because they are out in the daylight so much. For those who do need glasses, watching them return to school and show them off to their peers, pointing to leaves on trees and the writing on the blackboard that they can suddenly see, is heartening.

We're now working with our teachers to alert them to other eye-related issues and to teach them simple solutions, such as seating certain students in the front row or in well-lit areas of the classroom. Our teacher training sessions also train our teachers to encourage students to take care of their glasses and tell them the steps to take to ensure that those with more serious eye conditions receive the treatment they need.

One particular eye exam in early 2011 led to a further expansion of our health efforts. Savin, who was treating one of our students for a nasty-looking sty in her eye, realized in the course of the examination that the student was almost completely deaf. She had passed the vision test she had been given months earlier because it hadn't required any verbal communication. Her teacher had known about her hearing issue, but had assumed that nothing could be done to help.

We subsequently identified another deaf child in the class, and as students started to understand the situation they began to point out other children with similar problems. At least one child was fitted with a hearing aid, and another was admitted to the Krousar Thmey School in Siem Reap for blind and deaf children. We are now working with the International Medical Clinic (IMC) and organizations like All Ears Cambodia to do more.

We are also hoping for permission to begin bringing CFC students to AHC for dental care. We already have two dentists in Singapore who have expressed interest in helping.

One of our most interesting collaborations is with the IMC to measure the height and weight of each of our students and to record these and other vital statistics into a bilingual medical form. We've been able to compare the medical records to World Health Organization standards. Given the conditions in which they live, we weren't surprised to learn that our kids are comparatively stunted. In response, we've added more protein to our Food for Thought meals and are distributing vitamins, particularly A, zinc, and iron.

It will be interesting as time goes by to quantify any improvements against our earlier data and against WHO standards.

Kravaan School Comes of Age

Despite all these successes and the dramatic turnaround at the schools in Spien Chrieve, Bakong, Kong Much, and Aranh, the school in Kravaan remained a major thorn in our side.

While Kravaan retained a special place in my heart because it was the first school I visited with Srelin, it represented a challenge, largely because of its proximity to Angkor Wat and the other major temples.

Some of the school-age children like Srelin spend mornings at the temples hawking their wares and then go to school in the afternoon, but many others stay at the temples all day and don't go to school at all. At some level you have to respect the need for children to contribute to the family income in an impoverished country like Cambodia, but that need sometimes conflicts with CFC's mission to see that every child has the opportunity for a quality education.

The school's proximity to the main road to the temples and its visible location presents other problems as well. It means that the school is a popular stop for tour buses, an easy way to give foreigners an "inside look" at a real Cambodian school. Groups of foreigners wandering around the campus are disruptive to the learning experience. It also means the school hits the radar of various NGOs, and it is difficult to get a handle on who is doing what. In fact, a plaque on the outside of the building at Kravaan states that a man named Bob Ellis was responsible for the initial construction of the school. For years we asked people in the community who Bob Ellis was, but we could never get a satisfactory answer.

Then a few years ago Bob visited the school and I learned he was an American friend of Dr. Gene's who had visited Siem Reap as a tourist. Not unlike Bill and me, Bob and his wife Jane had been inspired to do something to help the children and had funded the school in Kravaan. Fortuitously, Dr. Gene introduced us, and when Bob and Jane saw what CFC was trying to do they became partners for change and huge CFC boosters.

This turned out to mark a turning point at Kravaan. CFC gradually began to take on more responsibility, and the people there really began to appreciate the changes CFC could make. Extending the Food for Thought program into Kravaan made a big difference, as did bringing in our teacher trainer and mentor teachers to help with curriculum development in traditional school subjects like math and history, and setting up a card catalogue and lending library system.

We also suggested strategies for tackling the school's high rate of absenteeism. For one thing, we laid down the law that any visit by tourists or an NGO had to be scheduled well in advance and had to be organized so as not to disrupt the school day. We didn't want strangers walking around campus unless they had a good reason for their visit and permission from the school's principal. We also assigned one of our best mentor teachers, Jenda, to talk to the teachers about our expectations for classroom management and how to take roll call so they could identify those students who showed up on a regular basis and those who did not. Jenda also helped teach students that truancy isn't in anyone's interests, isn't acceptable, and had to end.

After much diligent effort, we successfully brought Kravaan into the CFC fold. We organized a major campus cleanup and gave the buildings a new paint job inside and out. We also completely tore down two structures and replaced them with a new kindergarten building. We called it Little Orchard, after the preschool we had already established. Kravaan teachers now regularly attend CFC teacher training workshops, where they learn everything from how to create a lesson plan to how to design and decorate their classrooms so they are more conducive to learning.

The Floods of 2011

"It's always something" as the saying goes, and during the 2011 monsoon season our CFC schools, like the rest of Cambodia and most other Southeast Asian countries, experienced record floods.

In the end, more than 230,000 hectares of rice fields in Cambodia were destroyed, homes and streets were flooded, schools were closed, and at least 250 people died. The Cambodian government set aside significant funds for repairs, and relief efforts were organized from around the globe.

The flooding hit most of our schools and the surrounding communities at the beginning of October, just as the new academic year had begun. Roads became treacherous or impassable, and many students and faculty could not leave their homes because of the rising waters. Others stayed and desperately tried to keep the flooding at bay.

My nephew Anthony happened to be in Siem Reap during the floods, and he remembers seeing water everywhere as he pitched in to build barricades with pieces of banana trees, sand, and whatever else was on hand. He describes the scene vividly:

> The flooding was so bad, roads just collapsed. Potholes were everywhere. Sometimes they might be just a couple of inches deep, but then you'd hit one that ripped out the entire undercarriage of your car. You had to drive one or two miles per hour to be safe. The small market on the road and a couple of little restaurants tried to do

business with water up to the waiters' calves. The stilts holding up some of the houses weren't high enough, so people would be sleeping in their beds and roll over and flop into the water. And this wasn't clean water; there was fecal matter and dead livestock in it.

Despite our best efforts to place sandbags around the walls of our schools, water entered classrooms in Aranh, Kong Much, and Spien Chrieve. In Kravaan and Bakong we were able to start classes the first week of October, but our beautiful Aranh campus was hit the hardest. Even the eldest members of the community couldn't remember a comparable flood. At first temporary classes for primary school age children were held at the nearby monastery, but then the entire area, including the monastery, succumbed to flood waters and classes had to be cancelled altogether.

By this time, almost ten years into CFC changing the way teachers and students felt about school, neither group would accept defeat by the floods. In Aranh our CFC students took the lead in building a bridge over the flooded road by placing desks a few feet apart, then laying wooden planks between them.

Aranh flooded, a bridge made of desks. They want to go to school!

"They'd do anything to get to school," Anthony recalls. "Kids arrived in canoes and on scooters with plastic tubes crammed into the exhaust pipes to lift the fumes up above the water."

The waters began to recede toward the end of October, but as late as early November, two weeks after classes began, more than a foot of water remained in Aranh's first floor classrooms.

CFC responded to the crisis with an emergency fundraising campaign among our supporters in Singapore that allowed us to distribute rice and fish to about 120 families and pay for the tons of gravel we needed to repair the gardens and walkways on our campuses. As MAD volunteers worked alongside Cambodian volunteers to make the necessary repairs, we kept in mind ways we could better fortify our schools in preparation for the next catastrophic flood. Just like we were working to make our efforts to improve the teaching and health of our students sustainable into the indefinite future, we wanted the improvements in our infrastructure to "stand on their own" as well.

As our schools reopened, there was a singular bounce to the ceremonies in the same way that post-9/11 America experienced a burst of patriotic pride. At Bakong, for example, there was a special poignancy on the first day of school as many of the kindergarteners had a difficult time leaving their parents' sides. At the outdoor assembly, we watched them stare at the older students in order to mimic the correct form and spacing. The Cambodian flag was raised and the children gathered in straight lines near the flagpole to recite the pledge of allegiance and sing the national anthem. As announcements were made, the children listened, standing silently. On that first day of school after the floods, this routine, performed twice daily at all our schools, had a special meaning. I am certain the new kindergartens, who were then ushered into their spectacularly colorful classrooms, will never forget it.

While the new students were getting oriented, the rest of the school went on parade, marching two kilometers through the village and then looping back to school. They held banners high, proclaiming, "We will study for our family and for our country. We will improve ourselves to help develop our community!"

The Amelios Return to Texas

Our family's transition back to Texas has been challenging on many levels. There were so many unknowns, ranging from how each of us would adjust, to how I would maintain control over CFC's burgeoning responsibilities from nine thousand rather than eight hundred miles away.

Many of the goodbyes were difficult, for me none sadder than saying goodbye to our nanny, Mana, who returned home to Myanmar. During our ten years in Singapore Mana became part of our family, so much so that we even managed to turn her orange.

About midway through her decade living with us, on one of her trips home to see her family, she started helping out at a nearby school, donating rice and supplies. Her own family was as poor as any in our Cambodian villages, but eventually she started a school just outside her family's village, patterned after what she had heard over the years about Caring for Cambodia.

Watching Mana say goodbye to Avery was truly crushing, but that night as I lay in bed, I decided that if I had done nothing else in our ten years in Asia, I had inspired someone with absolutely no financial resources of her own to do something for others.

Fortunately, thanks to our email/Skype/plugged-in-world, the transition to running CFC from Texas went incredibly smoothly. The operations board definitely helped, and being in the states actually opened up new avenues, including a relationship with the Cambodian-American community in Austin. Not only that, but under Liz King's leadership, our Washington, DC chapter is now an important part of our fundraising and outreach efforts.

One of the people we partnered with is the Honorable Sichan Siv, former U.S. ambassador to the United Nations. Ambassador Siv was working for a U.S. relief agency in Cambodia in 1975 when the Khmer Rouge took over; he missed the last U.S. evacuation helicopter by thirty minutes while arranging food and medical supplies for some three thousand stranded refugee families. He was sent to a slave labor camp but miraculously escaped, arriving in Connecticut in 1976 when he was eighteen years old. Beginning with picking apples in rural New England, he pursued the American dream, capped off by his appointment as the ambassador to the United Nations by President George W. Bush.

I have had the honor of sharing the podium with Ambassador Siv on numerous occasions. Together we are spreading the message of how people everywhere can give Cambodians not a hand out, but a hand up, and truly help change lives.

Another member of our Washington, DC community is Narin Seng Jameson, who I met at a reception for CFC organized by the World Health Organization. She actually introduced me to Ambassador Siv. In 2010 CFC published *Cooking the Cambodian Way*, a cookbook by Narin that seeks to preserve the culture and tradition of Cambodian cooking as it has been done for generations.

To my great joy, back home in Austin I quickly learned that I need not feel totally estranged from the Asian roots that had grown within me during our ten years in Singapore. Some of my best new friends are Cambodian-Americans who have welcomed us into the Asian-American community and introduced us to new friends and their families. It has been an unexpected bonus to be able to spend time with people like Channy and Laura Seour and Savy and Kang Buoy, all of whom were orange even before I met them. They understand what is going on in Cambodia and have been immensely supportive. Another bonus to "coming home" is that Bill's best friend Pete Bartolotta and his family live just around the corner. Pete's wife Hope has become a great orange friend, another Austinite who is stepping up to the plate to help CFC stay strong, in her case making two trips to Siem Reap in the past two years.

On the personal front, we have a CFC family that continues to grow and expand. Samedi, the tour guide who first took Virginia, Amanda, and me to Angkor Wat and to the Kravaan School way back in 2003, attended his son's first day in the first grade in Spien Chrieve this past September. Several CFC teachers have now given birth, and Savy and Mum's son, Ung Dawson, is a happy, adorable little boy who will soon be attending one of our preschools. I don't know that I've ever felt more honored than when Savy and Mum asked me to name their son. I knew of their personal battle to have a child and I was ecstatic to help in some very small way.

All eight Amelios have adapted well to life back in Austin in the great state of Texas. Riley and Bronson are fiends for lacrosse, while Avery spends her after-school time with gymnastics and dance. Rathana and Cherry, now high school seniors, are into American music, movies, high school activities, and the stress of taking their SATs and applying to college. Their English, reflected in their ever-improving scholastic achievements, is amazing. Rathana plays lacrosse and is on the varsity cheerleading squad. Cherry is a terrific field hockey and softball player. They both still spend summers in Cambodia.

Unlike most other teenagers in America, Rathana and Cherry carry with them a unique story, a story of two families and a past so unlike my own or of their friends. I know this dual life and twin set of knowledge banks will propel them both to an exceptional future, whatever that might be.

Recently I asked Rathana what she tells her friends when they ask about CFC.

"I tell them that Caring for Cambodia is a bridge between two worlds, helping children walk across it," she told me. "It's not about putting children in a better position in life. It's about helping them, encouraging them to reach their dreams and hopes and goals and to achieve what they want with their life. I believe when you come into this world you are borrowing something. And when you give back, you've created a balance."

The most difficult part of returning to Austin has been the hole created by Virginia's absence. Austin is where we first met and where she helped me through so many difficult times. I miss her every single day.

Saving My Son Austin

Cambodia and CFC remain an enormous part of all our lives, but in the end Cambodia had the most profound impact on my eldest child. Who would have guessed? During those early visits, beginning when he was fourteen, I sometimes felt like I was dragging Austin to Siem Reap kicking and screaming. Now I see that those trips planted a seed that would not die and that just maybe, as he insists, saved his life.

Austin puts it this way:

> Even on my first trip to Cambodia I was struck by everything I saw. Around every corner I'd see something different than anything I'd ever experienced. Cambodia started to completely shatter the way I viewed everything. People would come up to me and ask, "Do you have a dollar?" and I'd be scrounging in my pockets thinking, "I want to help you, and you, and you, and you." But you realize you can't do it all. That was the most eye-opening thing, that these amazing people were trying to survive on a couple of rice bowls a day, yet still had smiles on their faces. And here I am, my family has given me more than anyone

in the world, and I'm struggling with addiction and doing all this partying. In Singapore, pretty much when you can walk, you can drink. I put my parents through a lot, as most teenagers do, but me a little more than most.

But then Austin would return to Singapore and go back to his old ways. Austin says he hit bottom during his freshman year at California Lutheran University, the first time he was ever truly on his own, during what he calls "the gnarliest year of my life." After his first semester in California he moved into an apartment so he would have no supervision whatsoever. Ten minutes from campus and nine thousand miles from his family, he was doing drugs and ended up in some legal trouble. Finally it became too much for him and he called to ask for help.

Bill and I were ready to put him back into rehab, although by now he was over eighteen so we couldn't legally force him to do anything. But we told him we wouldn't support him financially if he didn't get some help. The rest of us were in Texas for the summer, and Austin agreed to go to a rehab center as an outpatient five days a week for a month and then we'd make a decision as to whether or not the program was working. He ended up attending ninety Alcoholics Anonymous meetings in ninety days. For a time he did seem better.

"The AA meetings couldn't help but make an impression," Austin says. "Listening to all these crazy stories about people in their thirties, forties, and fifties whose lives had been ruined. Hearing about how they had lost their car, their job, their family."

Still, any lessons he took from AA, or from Cambodia for that matter, were not ready to stick.

Austin fell off the wagon again and spent the better part of the next two years going to school in Austin and "partying as hard as I could." Meanwhile, the best friend of another of Austin's cousins, Anthony's brother Nick, died of an overdose. That hit all of us hard and it scared me to death. Nick was in particularly bad shape, so I suggested to Austin that he and Nick go to Cambodia together for a couple of months. That proved to be Austin's turning point.

"We got up every day at the crack of dawn to help build one of the playgrounds," Austin remembers. "Verbal communication was impossible, except maybe a few words like, 'Hello Austin, wish you luck all the time.' I didn't even know what that meant, but somehow it meant more than what my friends in the States would say to me."

It helped that both his cousins, neither of whom are exactly teetotalers, had come to understand that Austin had an inability to drink in moderation.

Austin recalls his epiphany this way:

> We were getting up early to start work at 8:00 a.m. so we didn't have time to drink, except for maybe beer with dinner. Every night Nick and I would have these crazy philosophical talks. Looking back, every day for seven years had just been mayhem. Fear and loathing and weirdness all the time.
>
> Finally it was occurring to me that maybe it's not all about ME. My mom and dad had been presenting that to me year after year, but finally it was dawning on me what they were talking about. This time, working in Cambodia made me look at my life from a bird's eye view, almost like I was up in the clouds and looking down at my life in the States and seeing everything in this different perspective.
>
> Finally I asked myself, "What the hell am I doing?" All these people out here struggling to get food, to get clothes, going to the bathroom in the water that they swim in. And what am I doing with my life? Seeing on their

faces how thankful they were that two regular American dudes were over there helping helped me connect the dots.

I thought of my sisters too. I had watched these two girls come from eating crickets and little bowls of rice to getting an education at an international school. They were phenomenal. I don't go a day without thinking of the people in Siem Reap and how they live. On July 4, 2009, I returned to Singapore and I haven't had a drink since. Ironically, I got sober as soon as I was legal to drink.

When Austin returned to Texas he suddenly began taking school seriously. He decided he wanted to get a theatre arts degree, and we told him we'd take care of tuition if he could get into St. Edwards University, recognized by *U.S. News & World Report* as one of "America's Best Colleges." He had to make straight As his last semester at Austin Community College and he did it.

He graduated from St. Edwards last year.

"Maybe I needed all the other experiences, including the stints at rehab, to see my way clear of all the madness," says Austin. "But in the end it was Cambodia."

But in the end it was Cambodia.

For me too.

The Amelio sons.

APPENDIX A

Salary Bonus Criteria Observation Sheet

Teacher Evaluation: Salary Bonus Criteria
Observation Sheet

Name of Teacher: _____   Grade Level: _____

Name of School: _____

	Observation One Date:	Observation Two Date:	Observation Three Date:	Observation Four Date:	Observation Five Date:	Rating Scale of teacher performance: (1 being the lowest & 5 being the highest.)	Evaluator's comments:	Signatures:
Criteria One: *Teacher was in the class when observer arrived at school.*	☐ Yes ☐ No	☐ Yes ☐ No	☐ Yes ☐ No	☐ Yes ☐ No	☐ Yes ☐ No	1 2 3 4 5		Teacher: Evaluator:
Criteria Two: *Students were in class working quietly. Each student was engaged.*	☐ Yes ☐ No	☐ Yes ☐ No	☐ Yes ☐ No	☐ Yes ☐ No	☐ Yes ☐ No	1 2 3 4 5		Teacher: Evaluator:
Criteria Three: *Classroom was clean.*	☐ Yes ☐ No	☐ Yes ☐ No	☐ Yes ☐ No	☐ Yes ☐ No	☐ Yes ☐ No	1 2 3 4 5		Teacher: Evaluator

continued ▲

235

sixteen schools in Siem Reap. In 2005, 2010, and 2012 Jamie was awarded the prestigious Golden Hand Service Award by the Cambodian government. She is also the author of the children's book, *Stumpy the Crocodile*. After living in Asia for ten years, Jamie, her husband Bill, and their six children now live in Austin, Texas.

Christopher Graves, Director

Christopher Graves heads one of the world's leading public relations firms and serves on the board of its parent company, Ogilvy & Mather. Prior to being named global CEO, he served as CEO of Ogilvy PR in Asia Pacific. Graves joined Ogilvy PR after twenty-three years in business news, including eighteen years with Dow Jones and the *Wall Street Journal*. He was one of the founders of the *Wall Street Journal Report* and vice president in charge of news and programming for CNBC Asia and CNBC Europe.

Brent Nelson Smith, Director

Brent Nelson Smith is a co-founder and managing partner of LevelOne Capital Limited, providing financial advisory, consulting, investment, and business services throughout Asia, and is executive chairman of its subsidiary Vietnam Venture Group Limited. He was previously with DBS Bank Ltd, Southeast Asia's largest bank, where he was managing director and group head of corporate and investment banking, based in Singapore (2003–2007).

Elizabeth King, Director

Liz King has an MA from UC Berkeley in Educational Psychology and a BA from Middlebury College. She has been involved in the field of education for eighteen years as a teacher, tutor, curriculum developer, and consultant working in San Francisco, Washington, DC, and Singapore. She has been a volunteer with CFC since its founding and played a central role in the development of its teacher training program.

Cuong Do, Director

Cuong Do serves as senior vice president of corporate strategy and business development at TE Connectivity, one of the world's largest providers of products and solutions that connect and protect the flow of power and data in virtually every industry. With fiscal 2010 sales of U.S. $12.1 billion, TE Connectivity has approximately 100,000 employees in fifty countries.

Michael O'Neill, Secretary

Mr. O'Neill was appointed chief legal officer for CHC Helicopter on February 15, 2011. Previously Mr. O'Neill served as senior vice president and general counsel for the Lenovo Group, the global personal computer maker, where he was responsible for all legal, contracts, government affairs, and security for the company.

Joanne Leong Neidow, Treasurer

Joanne Leong Neidow resides in New York City with her husband Chris and their two children. She is a former vice president of Corporate Finance at American Express.

APPENDIX C

Blog by Liz King

(Originally posted on *www.mykidsupport.com* in January, 2010)

It's a familiar and heartwarming story: inspired individual raises funds to build a school in an impoverished country. Building projects are tangible. The cost is quantifiable. Buildings have completion dates, and when they are finished, the solid walls and fresh paint bring a sense of vitality and hope to a village. That's the feel-good picture.

But then what? If beautiful classrooms are not filled with great teachers and the resources needed to teach effectively, a spanking new building in a harsh climate—hot or cold—quickly morphs into an old-looking structure that can become a lasting symbol of dashed hopes or, worse, abandonment. Bricks and mortar alone are not enough.

Teacher training isn't a particularly sexy term in fundraising circles. Pictures of adults in classrooms don't tug at the heartstrings of potential donors the way a deserving child does. But in the end, what is an education for a child without great teachers at its center? This question is at the heart of one nonprofit's mission. That nonprofit's answer? Schools cannot excel without great teachers.

Seven years ago this month, I was part of a team of international classroom teachers based in Singapore asked to provide recommendations to the then newly established nonprofit Caring for Cambodia (CFC). CFC had sponsored three government primary schools in Siem Reap, Cambodia, within miles of the temples of Angkor Wat. The schools served three thousand of Cambodia's poorest children. CFC's founder, Jamie Amelio, started with bricks and mortar like so many, but she also had the vision and commitment to support these schools and their communities holistically and for the long haul. She sought input from, among others, practicing teachers.

We were not a team of educators with advanced degrees in international education or third world development, which some might argue would have been wise. What we had collectively was a lot of classroom teaching experience—close to a century, on three continents, in a wide range of educational settings. We did not know if this would be sufficient, but we were all committed to the challenge.

Our initial observations were stark. Cambodia remains one of the poorest countries in the world. Fifty percent of Cambodians in Siem Reap Province live below the poverty line. Students were malnourished and most came to school on an empty stomach. Classrooms had up to sixty students and virtually no teaching supplies. Most teachers sat at desks completing paperwork rather than teaching. Perhaps most shocking was that those classes of sixty children sat quietly in rows, impeccably behaved.

Our team learned that attending government schools in Cambodia came with hidden costs to these students' families, most of whom supported their families on less than thirty U.S. dollars a month. Students were required to wear uniforms that were not provided for free. Teachers received government salaries inconsistently (sometimes going several months without a paycheck), so there was an unspoken agreement that students were to bring money to school each day to ensure their teachers would show up. Families were making significant financial sacrifices for their children to attend school, so on some level we knew they valued education.

As a result of these observations, our essential recommendation was twofold: feed the school community and focus on teachers. Feeding the school community was the more straightforward of the two. To address this issue, CFC established Food for Thought, a program with a two-pronged strategy for addressing malnutrition in the school communities. Under the program, CFC each day provides students with healthy, balanced meals to ensure they can think about learning, not hunger. Longer term, CFC provides parent education in health and nutrition, arming village adults with knowledge to break the cycle of chronic malnutrition. To deliver the program, CFC serves local produce that is prepared by parent volunteers and paid local cooks, channeling much-needed support into the grassroots economy.

Focusing on the teachers was more complex. Cambodia presents an unusual set of circumstances. Between 1975 and 1979, an estimated 1.7 million Cambodians were executed, starved, or killed by disease at the hands of the Khmer Rouge. Most of those executed were professionals and intellectuals, among them nearly all of Cambodia's teachers. Forty years later, Cambodia is still recovering from this unimaginable loss. The educational system is certainly no exception.

One CFC teacher, Chan Vandy, provides a typical teacher's biography in some respects. She was born in 1980, just after the fall of the Khmer Rouge. "My parents had worked so long and hard during the Khmer Rouge that they could no longer work. We had little food and barely survived. It is hard to talk about."

Chan Vandy began school at age six. "At that time we did not have teachers or schools like today. A village woman would gather children together under a tree and we sat on rocks. The teacher had a blackboard and used clay as chalk. We learned basic things."

Unlike her contemporaries, only nine percent of whom completed secondary education, Chan Vandy remained in school through secondary school. She also completed one year of teacher training "college" in a country where, according to 2007 UNESCO statistics, only five percent of the post secondary-aged population enrolls in post secondary education. She had no mentors. An entire generation of teachers with experience was missing.

If anyone can help turn around a school in Cambodia, Chan Vandy can. In addition to an unrelenting pride in her country, she has a resolute determination to see her country's schools improve. She has newly adopted government curriculum documents on a shelf in her classroom that set lofty, internationally recognized goals for her Cambodian students, goals that if met will enable her students to work and raise families above the poverty line.

She also has traits vital to great teaching. New research from the nonprofit Teach for America suggests that more than any other variable in education—more than schools or curriculum—teachers matter. With that reality in mind, Teach for America has studied the nation's most effective teachers, nearly all of whom teach in underserved, urban schools in the U.S., and identified six common qualities among them. Effective teachers:

1. Set big goals for students
2. Routinely reevaluate their teaching and its effectiveness
3. Seek the involvement of students and families in the process
4. Remain focused on student learning
5. Plan exhaustively and purposefully for each school day

6. Work relentlessly despite obstacles such as poverty, bureaucracy, and lack of funds

But what CFC has recognized is that while great potential teachers like Chan Vandy exist in Cambodia, the prevailing means of teacher training have not been sufficiently effective. CFC also recognizes that stepping into a foreign country and making recommendations about how best to give teachers the hard skills necessary to educate their students is tough and requires, above all else, acute cultural awareness and appreciation.

Schools prepare citizens. As a result, the content and delivery of one country's curriculum is not one-size-fits-all for another. With that reality in mind, CFC has established a culturally relevant teacher-training program that is a unique cornerstone of the organization's work. Unlike large top-down training projects where funding depends on the number of teachers reached (usually necessitating a large seminar format), CFC works from the ground up, keeping training sessions small, "hands on," and directly applicable to the goals of Cambodia's curriculum. Teachers are taken through a consistent, systematic learning process with each new skill presented. If, for example, they are being trained to read aloud to students, first they will observe a trainer read, then they will practice reading to trainers posing as students, then they will read to a class of students jointly with a trainer, and finally they will read to a class independently. It's a method better known in teaching circles as "I do, we do, you do"—a lesson flow great teachers know well.

More than one hundred international teachers, most based in Singapore, have participated in CFC's teachers-training-teachers project. Most critical, CFC raised funds to create a full-time, in-country director of teacher training staff position currently held by a master teacher from New Zealand with more than thirty years of classroom teaching experience both at home and abroad. She oversees the development of all training workshops, but her expertise is most powerful when shared on a daily basis in the form of individualized support and mentorship to the ninety-five CFC teachers with whom she works.

How does CFC measure the success of its teachers? One way is through the growing popularity of its schools. CFC now supports five government schools, including a secondary school, serving a total 5,300 students. One of these schools is positioned as a "model school" and receives frequent visits from Ministry of Education officials interested in observing Cambodia's newly revised curriculum and "child friendly" standards in action.

The level of professionalism among CFC teachers across all five schools is rising. Teachers are paid regularly according to a performance-based salary system with clearly defined expectations they helped establish. Newly installed classroom shelves hold locally purchased supplies and teaching resources developed by teachers with the guidance of mentors. For the first time, classrooms have bulletin boards made with indigenous materials that display student work.

Improvements in the primary school environment have also generated interest among village mothers in creating village preschools. Interested mothers receive early childhood training so that they can become their children's first teachers. CFC's pilot pre-school opened March 31, 2009, with thirteen mothers participating. Less than one year later, forty-eight mothers are signed up for training. Families want to be involved.

Perhaps most notably, Chan Vandy and several of her colleagues have joined the ranks of CFC's teacher trainers, training not only fellow CFC teachers but also teachers from neighboring government schools eager for inspiration and support. These exemplary teachers have been given the opportunity to travel to Singapore and observe international classrooms at work. They take what they see and make it relevant for their own students.

CFC is like the proverbial stone that has been dropped into a pond, creating rings of influence radiating outward. This cascading effect is at the heart of what makes CFC's training model sustainable. CFC's near-term teacher training goal is clear: to train Cambodian teachers to be teacher trainers capable of directing CFC's teacher training project. Chan Vandy and her colleagues agree that they are not quite there yet, but the goal is well within reach. Once that goal is met, the stage will be set for a lifelong professional collaboration among a growing circle of international teachers, all of whom strive for nothing less than educational excellence. What could be more encouraging? After all, more than any other variable in education . . . teachers matter.

APPENDIX D:

Signature Phrases, or "Orange-isms"

- Orange moment
- Turning orange
- The critical few versus the trivial many
- A lightning bolt of emotion
- A gift of burden
- Giving a hand up, not a hand out
- Looking for more than money . . . looking for hope
- Sustainable and scalable
- Education . . . the key to everything.
- We didn't know what we didn't know.
- When it comes to expanding our efforts, it's better to go deep than wide.
- Talk less, do more.
- Don't promise anything you can't deliver.
- How do you measure hope?
- Together, let's see it through.

- As one person, I cannot change the world, but I can change the world of one person.
- To whom much is given, much is expected.